Cultural Change in Family Firms

Anticipating and Managing Business and Family Transitions

W. Gibb Dyer, Jr.

Cultural Change in Family Firms

Anticipating and Managing Business and Family Transitions

Jossey-Bass Publishers

San Francisco • London • 1986

CULTURAL CHANGE IN FAMILY FIRMS
Anticipating and Managing Business and Family Transitions
W. Gibb Dyer, Jr.

Copyright © 1986 by: Jossey-Bass Inc., Publishers
433 California Street
San Francisco, California 94104
&
Jossey-Bass Limited
28 Banner Street
London EC1Y 8QE

Library of Congress Cataloging-in-Publication Data

Dyer, W. Gibb (date)
    Cultural change in family firms.

    (The Jossey-Bass management series) (The Jossey-Bass
social and behavioral science series)
    Bibliography: p. 167
    Includes index.
    1. Family corporations—Management.   2. Corporate
culture.   I. Title.   II. Series.   III. Series:
Jossey-Bass social and behavioral science series.
HD62.25.D94   1986   658'.045   86–10585
ISBN 1–55542–007–9 (alk. paper)

Manufactured in the United States of America

The paper in this book meets the guidelines for
permanence and durability of the Committee on
Production Guidelines for Book Longevity of the
Council on Library Resources.

JACKET DESIGN BY WILLI BAUM

FIRST EDITION

Code 8634

A joint publication in
The Jossey-Bass Management Series
and
The Jossey-Bass
Social and Behavioral Science Series

Consulting Editors
Management of Family-Owned Businesses

Richard Beckhard
Richard Beckhard Associates

Peter Davis
The Wharton School
University of Pennsylvania

Barbara Hollander
The Family Firm Institute

A Note to the Reader

Over 95 percent of all businesses in the United States are family owned. Although many family businesses are small, a substantial proportion are major corporations, including about 175 of the *Fortune* 500. Family businesses produce almost half the gross national product and generate about 50 percent of the total wages paid in this country. The effectiveness of such companies and the quality of their management are clearly significant for the economy and the society.

Family business is without doubt the predominant form of organization in the modern economy, yet little has been written about it until recently. Interest in the subject is growing dramatically, partly because large numbers of founders who established their businesses after World War II now face retirement. These entrepreneurs are vitally interested in succession planning. In addition, many younger people are entering their families' businesses because they see opportunities to advance rapidly and to make a more significant impact than they could in nonfamily firms. Moreover, entrepreneurial starts increased from 90,000 in 1951 to 900,000 in 1984. A large number of these are or will become family firms. With this economic shift toward entrepreneurialism, the welfare of the family firm is more important than ever.

Family businesses tend to have relatively short life spans, averaging twenty-four years. Problems such as succession, the interplay of family issues and business decisions, the professional development of family members, the transition to nonfamily management, the retention of competent nonfamily employees, and the balance of personal and corporate finances are all factors that make the survival of the family firm perilous.

ix

New information about family-owned firms has emerged in recent years from such diverse fields as family theory and therapy, sociology, psychology, business, organizational behavior and development, finance, and law. The family firm is now recognized as a highly complex entity involved in a system composed of three major parts—the family, the business, and the marketplace. Events in one part of the system, we now know, are likely to have ramifications for other parts.

The Jossey-Bass series on management of family-owned businesses is dedicated to providing readers with practical, applicable state-of-the-art information about these businesses. It is designed primarily for people actually involved in family businesses—owners, managers (both family and nonfamily), and board members—who are committed to increasing their firms' effectiveness. Each book will examine new concepts in the management of family firms and will support the systematic development of knowledge and skills managers need to develop healthy family businesses.

Factors critical to the survival of the family business will be addressed—such as understanding family dynamics and their effects on the business, planning for succession, implementing strategic decision-making methods, selecting and managing employees, developing the culture of the organization, ensuring continuity, providing for career development within the company, and developing and utilizing a board of directors. While many of these ideas have been addressed in other more general books, this series will consider each one in the unique context of the family firm, where family issues and business concerns overlap.

Books in the series will also be of value to professionals who serve family firms: accountants, lawyers, family therapists, financial planners, bankers, and management consultants. An individual in any one of these areas may find it difficult to cope with the complexities of a family firm's mode of operation. Accountants, for example, often report frustration when the emotional processes of the family impinge on their work with the business. This series of books will enable such professionals to increase their familiarity with all areas that relate to family business matters and to identify resources for handling those not within their purview.

Academics, students, and researchers will also find this series useful. To date, the literature and research has been sparse, particularly in light of the numbers of family firms in the United States and their impact on the economy. There are, for example, no texts available on the family business. Several universities now offer courses on the family business, however, and research on the topic is increasing. In response to obvious need, we hope that the Jossey-Bass series on family business will serve as a foundation for researchers, students, professors, and professionals who are exploring theory and developing applications that will enhance the family-held business as a distinct economic form.

The series editors, all of whom have been both consultants to and researchers on family businesses, have identified the main topics the series will treat and have recruited experts to write on them. It is our hope that this series will become a significant and useful resource for all who are dedicated to ensuring the effectiveness of the family-owned business.

July 1986

Richard Beckhard
New York, New York

Peter Davis
Philadelphia, Pennsylvania

Barbara Hollander
Pittsburgh, Pennsylvania

Preface

Despite the importance of family-owned firms in the economies of the world, little systematic study of the dynamics of these enterprises has been undertaken, and few books and articles have discussed the often complex problems facing the manager of a family firm. Because they lack information concerning what works and what does not work, managers of family firms frequently have difficulty coping with problems such as creating a viable business, selecting and training family members for employment, managing conflicts within the family, and planning for succession. Thus they may make serious mistakes that could have been avoided if they had been more aware of the consequences of their actions. Because the findings presented here are based on more than forty in-depth case studies of family firms, *Cultural Change in Family Firms* will help the reader to understand and anticipate the kinds of problems leaders and managers of family firms encounter as the business and the family grow and mature. We think this knowledge will help managers handle those problems more effectively. Moreover, by giving the reader an inside look at the core beliefs, conflicts, and power struggles that form the cultures of family firms, the reader will gain an appreciation for the contribution these cultures make to the success of the family and the business.

Although research based, *Cultural Change in Family Firms* was written primarily for those who lead and manage family firms, for it suggests a number of practical applications of the studies' findings. Based on the experiences of successful and unsuccessful family firms, this book provides guidelines for coping with the difficult problems leaders of family firms encounter as their businesses and families develop. Consultants and therapists working with family firms, nonfamily managers working in family firms, and academics or business students interested in understanding the dynamics of these enterprises should also find the book useful.

My interest in family firms began a number of years ago when I was a new doctoral student at the Massachusetts Institute of Technology. Over lunch one day, Richard Beckhard asked me what I knew about family-owned businesses. "Not much," I replied, although I vaguely remembered that my grandfather had owned a small grocery store in Portland, Oregon, and that my father had spent a considerable amount of time in his youth helping him run the business. To my reply, Beckhard said, "That seems to be a real problem. There doesn't seem to be much research on family firms at all. However, many of my consulting clients are owners of family businesses, and the problems of managing both a family and a business simultaneously are enormous."

This discussion initiated our study of family firms. Beckhard and I invited leaders of family businesses from around the world to come to the Massachusetts Institute of Technology to share their problems with us in family firm conferences. We also began to gain access to family firms and to study them in-depth. From these experiences of studying and working with leaders of family firms, I came to understand firsthand the difficult, and often painful, issues they must confront each day.

While at the Massachusetts Institute of Technology, I also began studying organizational culture with Edgar H. Schein. As I applied the concept of culture to my study of family firms, I discovered that it helped me understand the dynamics of these complex enterprises. Many of the ideas in this book are a result of my early collaboration with both Beckhard and Schein.

In general, a family firm is an organization in which decisions regarding its ownership or management are influenced by a relationship to a family (or families). In some family firms, ownership and management are totally in the hands of a single family. In others there is only partial control of these two key factors. For example, Thomas Watson never owned IBM outright, but he was able to dominate management and promote his two sons to important leadership positions. Another type of family firm is the absentee-owned firm. Although the owning family makes all decisions regarding ownership, nonfamily managers are charged with running the business. A final category of family firm is the latent family firm. In these organizations a family member directs the business but other members of the family have no visible relationship to the business. However, as time passes and the leaders' children mature, they begin to want family involvement; thus the nature of the relationship between family and firm changes quickly. In some cases, the leader may unconsciously make decisions based on family concerns and needs. Thus, the business may appear to lack family involvement when the family connection is in fact quite strong.

To study this variety of family firms and compare and contrast their evolutionary patterns and cultures, my research assistants and I gathered historical data from more than forty family businesses. By using a historical approach much like the ones described by Mintzberg and Waters (1982) and Pettigrew (1979), we were able to intensively and systematically explore the different problems leaders of family businesses face at various stages of the family firm life cycle. We gathered data from a variety of sources including interviews with owners and managers of family firms, internal documents (for example, memos, newsletters, and minutes of board of director meetings), the memoirs of leaders of family businesses, corporate histories, and case studies published in a variety of newspapers and business journals. Because the leaders of family businesses are usually very secretive regarding the operation of their enterprises, we had to look to a variety of sources to complete the picture of the firms we studied. The firms range from such giants as Du Pont to small mom-and-pop operations. Even the large corporations, however, had very humble beginnings, and the founders and families that started those firms encountered many of the same problems that family businesses face today. By studying these large firms in retrospect and over long periods of time, we can achieve a greater understanding of the dynamics of family firms at various developmental stages.

We chose the firms we did because we had access to information regarding them. About one-half of our sample were open cases, inasmuch as most of the data were gathered from public sources. The identity of other firms has been disguised because the family wanted the data kept confidential. Although the majority of firms we studied were located in the United States, our sample of firms also included businesses in Europe, Central America, South America, and the Far East. The findings of our study are thus not entirely "culture bound" to the United States.

We tended to focus on successful family firms, since corporate histories or other documents were generally available. Unfortunately, few business historians are interested in firms that fail—unless, of course, they are spectacular failures. Despite these methodological shortcomings, the effects of the cultures in these firms were so consistent that the implications are clear: To compete in a dynamic and often uncertain world, managers of family businesses must be aware of their cultures and must be skilled at managing cultural change.

Overview of the Contents

Cultural Change in Family Firms consists of three parts. Part One, "The Evolution of Culture in Family Firms," is composed of three chapters that are largely descriptive. Chapter One describes the stages in the evolutionary cycle of the family firm and suggests that the culture of the family firm largely determines its ability to survive. Chapter Two defines the concept of culture and outlines the cultural patterns found in the business, the family, and the board of directors, describes how they relate to one another to form the cultural configuration of a family firm, and examines how these patterns evolve over time. In Chapter Three, the process of cultural change is outlined, including the role of leadership and the damaging effects of "revolutionary" change.

Part Two, "Anticipating Cultural Transitions from Generation to Generation," describes the key problems that may occur during various stages of development: during the founder's tenure, in the second and third generations, and when the family firm goes public or brings in professional managers. The problems of the founder culture are described in Chapter Four. The personal characteristics of the founder often lead to cultural patterns that may threaten the firm's survival. These cultural patterns, the problems they generate, and possible solutions to those problems are detailed in this chapter. Chapter Five discusses the conflicts that frequently arise in second- and third-generation family firms and the mechanisms for managing these conflicts. Chapter Six describes the cultural implications for those few family firms that do go public or bring in professional management. Both leaders of family firms and professional managers of family businesses should find this chapter useful.

The final part, "Managing Family Firms Successfully and Ensuring Continuity," describes what it takes to succeed in a family firm and how to manage the change process. Chapter Seven is probably the most important chapter in the book, for it outlines the attributes of those family firms that have made successful transitions between generations. Chapter Eight describes the steps in the change process: gathering data to decipher the culture of a family firm; detecting problems; and selecting, implementing, and evaluating various strategies for managing change. Consultants to family businesses and managers interested in the topic of change will find this chapter to be of particular interest. Finally, Chapter Nine lists the twelve major pitfalls to be avoided by leaders of family firms and describes how leaders can manage both continuity and change simultaneously.

Acknowledgments

Numerous individuals have contributed to this book. Richard Beckhard, Peter Davis, and Barbara Hollander, editors of this series of books on family firms, have provided me with encouragement and with many useful insights that helped frame and shape the book. William G. Dyer, Edgar H. Schein, and John Ward read earlier drafts of the manuscript and made suggestions that helped the book immeasurably.

My research team at Brigham Young University consisting of Jean Brown, Kathy Buckner, Alan Checketts, and Roger Peay contributed by gathering data on a number of family firms and writing working papers on various problems encountered by family firms. A number of M.B.A. research teams at Brigham Young University also gathered data used in this study. Paul Thompson, dean of the School of Management at Brigham Young University, and Gene Dalton, department chairman, helped to secure the necessary research funds and supported my research effort. My colleagues in the Department of Organizational Behavior have also critiqued certain parts of the book and have been very supportive. These people have made writing this book a much easier task.

Finally, I would like to thank my wife, Theresa Franck Dyer, for her help and support in making this book a reality. She read and provided useful comments on each draft of the book. She and our four children—Emily, Justin, Alison, and Mary—have helped me to understand some of the problems faced by people who attempt to manage a professional career and a family at the same time. It is to them this book is dedicated.

Provo, Utah   W. Gibb Dyer, Jr.
July 1986

Contents

The Author

W. Gibb Dyer, Jr., is an assistant professor of organizational behavior at Brigham Young University. He received both his B.S. degree (1977) in psychology and his M.B.A. degree (1979) from Brigham Young University; his Ph.D. degree (1984) in organization studies was awarded by the Massachusetts Institute of Technology. His primary research interests are in the areas of organizational culture, family-owned businesses, entrepreneurship, and managing change. He has served as a consultant for a number of organizations—both family and nonfamily businesses—on such issues as assessing organizational culture, managing cultural change, succession and human resource planning, and managing conflict. He has coauthored articles on family firms and on organizational culture that have appeared in *Organizational Dynamics, Sloan Management Review,* and *Personnel.*

Cultural Change in Family Firms

Anticipating and Managing Business and Family Transitions

Part One

The Evolution of
Culture in Family Firms

As we studied the histories of a number of family firms, it became clear that these firms go through significant changes as they evolve, and that these changes appear in patterns. Part One attempts to describe, in some detail, these evolutionary patterns. With the first three chapters, we hope to provide a greater understanding of how family firms develop, what kind of cultures are found in them, and how they change over time. Part One provides the context and background for what follows in the next two parts.

In Chapter One, a model of the family firm "life cycle" is described. This model suggests that the problems of family firms change as the business—and the family—move through their "infancy" to more mature forms. Leaders of family firms must be prepared to handle different sets of problems over time. The role of culture in managing change and successful transitions is also introduced.

Chapter Two describes the kind of business, family, and board cultures found in the family firms we studied. This configuration of business, family, and board cultures is the key to understanding the dynamics of family firms. To give the reader some of the "flavor" of these cultures, we present a number of rather detailed case studies that illustrate each type.

The role of leadership in changing culture is the topic of Chapter Three. The dynamics of culture change are described in the six stages of the "cycle of cultural evolution." This cycle indicates that family firms often go through traumatic crises and revolutionary changes because their leaders are not prepared. Implications for managing culture change are outlined.

1

One

How Culture Affects the
Firm's Growth and Development

The family firm has traditionally played a dominant role in our economy. More than 90 percent of U.S. businesses are classified as being family controlled, meaning that decisions about their management or ownership are influenced by a family. These "family firms" account for about one-half of all the country's jobs and a significant percentage (around 40 percent) of the gross national product (Danco, 1982). Hundreds of new businesses are being started each day, many of them family firms.

Still, despite the prominence of family firms in the economies of the world, they lead a tenuous existence. Few survive more than a few years, and fewer still are able to walk the delicate line between success in business and family relationships. The diverse and complex problems that leaders of family firms face as they attempt to manage a growing business and maintain harmony in their own families make survival difficult. One report indicates that fewer than one-third survive into the second generation (Poe, 1980).

It seems clear that family firms, in their growth from infancy to mature businesses, go through an evolutionary process with predictable patterns. In this evolution, business leaders find themselves constantly confronting new and unanticipated challenges, as both their firms and their families grow and mature. When they fail to anticipate these challenges, major problems emerge. Sometimes these problems are so severe, so unsolvable, that the firm dies. However, there is much that managers of family firms *can* do to ensure the survival of the business and the well-being of the family. Let us start with understanding the "typical" life cycle of the family firm.

3

The Standard Life Cycle

Over the history of a family firm, the issues requiring executive action change dramatically at different stages (Greiner, 1972; Adizes, 1979; Hershon, 1975). Based on the family firms we studied, there appear to be four common developmental stages in the family firm life cycle.

Stage 1: Creating the Business. In Stage 1, the founder, who is in the process of creating a new venture, is consumed with the problems of finding capital, developing a viable product, and creating the means for getting the product to the marketplace. Finding competent employees to staff a new enterprise is no small feat, so little thought is given to the wisdom of involving family members in the business: if they are willing and able, they are asked to join. Problems like leadership succession are something for the distant future—nothing to be too concerned about now. Survival is utmost in the founder's mind.

Stage 2: Growth and Development. As the business grows and matures, the founder must cope with a different set of problems. Changes in the business environment often force the family to make major strategic changes to maintain a competitive advantage. In a growing business, founders also begin to realize that they can no longer manage all facets of the business; they must begin to delegate responsibility and share power. As their work force grows, founders become concerned with teaching their own business values and beliefs to employees and passing those values on to succeeding generations. Decisions about training family and nonfamily members for future leadership become more pressing. We often find intense competition among family and nonfamily employees for leadership positions in Stage 2. Finally, retirement, estate planning, and the distribution of ownership and wealth become key issues in planning for leadership transitions. Most founders are not equipped to handle this diverse set of problems, and so few family businesses make it to the second generation.

Stage 3: Succession to the Second Generation. Family firms that evolve into Stage 3 experience problems that are quite different from those in earlier stages. The family and the business have now matured. The founder is no longer the dominant force; the firm has become a complex enterprise of family members, nonfamily employees, and perhaps outside investors. They all have diverse interests. For example, some family members may want to continue to put money back into the business, while others would like to have the profits distributed in the form of dividends. Issues surrounding ownership and equity are the principal cause of harmful conflicts in the second generation. In a climate of conflict, the family may also have to make strategic changes in the business to remain competitive and develop plans for training future managers. Given these dynamics, the major challenge facing Stage 3 firms is to manage conflict and bring people with diverse interests together to work for the common good.

Stage 4: Public Ownership and Professional Management. If a family firm survives the problems posed at the first three stages of development, it may again encounter a different set of problems. In Stage 4 the business needs additional capital to continue operation, and therefore the family must decide whether to go public. Bringing in professional management might also be necessary if there are not enough competent family members to manage the business. Only a small fraction of family firms reach this stage of development; many that have attempted to make this transition have faltered badly. Often at this stage the family firm ceases to exist, and the company becomes a publicly owned, professionally managed enterprise.

The Brown Corporation: A Life Cycle Model

To illustrate how the problems facing an evolving family business change as it moves through the various stages, let us briefly examine the history of one highly successful family firm.

A few blocks south of Main Street, in the small town of Orangeville, sit the green and white buildings of the Brown Corporation—the lifeblood of the community (all names are fictional). The company employs more than 500 people and brings $14 million in payroll into the valley each year. Because of the company's pervasive influence, Orangeville residents see themselves living in a "company town." They know their livelihood and that of residents of surrounding communities depend on the fortunes of the Brown Corporation.

Orangeville was founded in 1792. Although the first settlers in the valley were primarily farmers, as the village grew, craftsmen and artisans began to found small businesses. One of the most prominent of these new businesses was the English Iron Works, founded by Wilbur English and his family in 1840—a gray-iron foundry, machine shop, and planing mill. Iron ore and coal were shipped to Orangeville from Pennsylvania, and the finished products—a variety of agricultural equipment for the valley's farmers—were delivered to customers by barge or horse-drawn carriage. The iron works prospered for eighty years but ran into increasing financial difficulties in the early 1920s. Sales and profits dropped precipitously, and the English family, who had owned the business for three generations, began looking for a potential buyer. They happened to find just the right person in John Brown, Sr., a salesman with whom they had done business for some time.

Stage 1: Creating the Business. John Brown, Sr., was born in 1889 in a small town a few miles from Orangeville. Trained as an industrial engineer at a local college, he had worked in sales for a number of firms. Although he began his career working for others, John had one goal in mind: he wanted to own and manage his own business. When he heard that the English family was trying to sell its business, he borrowed money from his brother-in-law, found some additional financing from a partner, and bought the faltering iron works for $6,000 in 1922.

Like many entrepreneurs, John, Sr., had a particular philosophy of doing business. His creed had at its core more than twenty "rules," but the essence was hard work, a zest for innovation, and fair play in business dealings. John, Sr., carried out his vision with great zeal; he generally worked seven days a week and often called his subordinates on Sunday to prepare them for the upcoming week's activities. Following this philosophy, the company's sales boomed during the Roaring Twenties, reaching over $100,000 by 1929. The number of employees grew from a handful in 1922 to 100 by 1929.

However, the stock market crash in the fall of that year pushed the company to the brink of disaster. One by one, employees had to be let go until only three people remained—John, Sr.; his trusted assistant, Tim Henson; and a part-time secretary. For eight months in 1932 they were the entire work force. During this period John, Sr., and his family spent many an afternoon driving their Model-T Ford around the valley, drumming up business and settling old accounts.

Stage 2: Growth and Development. In the 1930s, under the direction of Tim Henson, the company began to develop a number of new products. Hydraulic pumps and lifting equipment could be made at the foundry, and John, Sr., began to see a growing market in this area. The advent of World War II brought increasing demand for lifting and material-handling equipment. The company prospered. By 1945 sales had reached $425,000 and the work force had increased to sixty.

The early 1940s were not easy for John, Sr., however. His absentee partner suddenly died and the partner's wife, who inherited his stock, demanded to be seated on the board of directors. Up until this time John, Sr., and his wife had dominated the board. A bitter fight developed over control of the company, and a number of lawsuits followed. Finally the case was settled out of court in 1945. John, Sr., paid his partner's widow $35,000 for her stock, vowing never to let outsiders gain control of his company.

John, Sr., had two children—John, Jr., and Elaine. Both spent many hours at the company—working weekends and summers, doing odd jobs and bookkeeping. When John, Jr., returned from military service in 1946, John, Sr., began grooming him for president. After just one year, John, Jr., was promoted to sales manager. The other employees viewed that as a rather quick advancement, but they never questioned the boss's prerogative to promote his son. Elaine's husband, Ralph, also worked in the business as assistant to John, Sr. There was no rivalry between the two younger men, however, since Ralph was generally seen as lacking leadership abilities; he had a history of mental illness, and often had to be "taken care of" by the family.

In the late 1940s revenues grew rapidly. A new material-handling truck developed by the company's chief engineer increased sales almost twofold. All seemed to be going well. Then in November of 1948 John, Sr., underwent emergency surgery to remove his appendix. While recovering from this operation, he had an attack of pancreatitis; he was given little chance to live. The family was panic-stricken. John, Sr., had made no preparations for such an event: his estate was not established, and no one was yet prepared to take over the business. With all these uncertainties, the Brown family was grimly prepared to sell the business should John, Sr., die.

But, miraculously, he began to recover. Although he was incapacitated for almost a year, John, Sr., began once again to be involved in the firm's affairs. But his involvement would never be the same. On the advice of his doctor, he began to spend the winters in Florida. The firm entered a transition period that was to last ten years.

John, Sr., was characterized by company employees as a "benevolent autocrat." He made all the major decisions, down to approving all capital expenditures over $50. He and his wife, who kept the company books, kept all important information about the firm in the family. But John, Sr., also took care of his employees, creating a familylike atmosphere in the firm. He took his key employees on fishing trips, sponsored a clambake for company employees and their families, and was noted for helping employees with various work and family problems. As he became less involved in the firm's activities, however, the nature of the company slowly began to change. In 1956, primarily for tax advantages and to raise capital, the company's stock was offered for sale to the public. Although the family retained well over 50 percent of the stock, an outsider, the family banker, was added to the board of directors for the first time.

Stage 3: Succession to the Second Generation. In contrast to his father, John, Jr., believed that workers should participate in decision making. His wife had attended a sensitivity training group sponsored by the Young Presidents Organization in 1960, and returned full of enthusiasm for the principles of trust, openness, and participation. John, Jr., decided to investigate and found himself attending a similar group. From this experience, he began to develop his own vision of the firm—a participative culture where all members of the organization, regardless of position, would be able to influence decisions. He began to enlist a number of behavioral science consultants to help him implement the new philosophy. Although many old-timers were bewildered by this dramatic change, the company continued to prosper; sales climbed from $6 million in 1960 to over $40 million in the early 1970s. John, Sr., was able to witness much of this growth. He died in 1967, having seen his small iron works transformed into a major corporation in the space of forty-five years.

Stage 4: Public Ownership and Professional Management. The Arab oil embargo and energy crisis in 1973 and 1974 provided the Brown Corporation with its first major crisis since the Great Depression. Sales slumped and inventories rose dramatically. To turn things around, the board of directors encouraged John, Jr., to bring in a manufacturing and inventory control specialist. They found just such a person in Reed Larson, an experienced manufacturing manager who worked at a large company a few miles from Orangeville.

Larson was seen as a competent, albeit acerbic, manager. Trained under Harold Geneen at International Telephone and Telegraph, Larson knew what it meant to shake things up and turn a company around. He immediately fired or demoted half of the manufacturing supervisors—he said they were "dead wood"—and implemented a modern inventory control system. In 1975, sales increased by $5 million, while manufacturing costs actually dropped by over $1 million. Output per hour also increased by 40 percent. Reed Larson's management style also greatly affected the participative culture of the Brown Corporation. Larson was rarely open to suggestions from his subordinates, whom he intimidated. The shop workers nicknamed him "Jaws" because of his tough demeanor. Larson hired other professional managers who fit his style. They competed intensely among themselves for advancement and often attempted to eliminate company traditions started by the family that they considered wasteful and inefficient.

During this period in the company's history, the Brown family also experienced a number of changes. John, Jr.'s oldest son, John III, nicknamed Mike, came to work for the company. In his early years Mike had not wanted to be in the family business. He tried to avoid the "little rich kid" stereotype by refusing to take any business classes in school. As a teenager, he took construction jobs in the summer. In college he majored in psychology, but his plans for a career in that field were interrupted by a traumatic divorce. He came back to Orangeville, eventually remarried, and started working at the company as a rather low-level technician. He deliberately avoided positions with any management responsibility, an attitude that caused frequent conflicts with his father. John, Jr.'s second son, Jim, also joined the business. Jim had returned to Orangeville from a stint in the Air Force and had earned an M.B.A. degree from a local college. Jim was interested in pursuing a managerial career and quickly advanced to a senior position in the company while Mike remained a technician. John's third child, Irene, obtained a degree in computer science and worked at a company a few hundred miles from the Brown Corporation. She, too, was interested in a management role in the company. John, Jr.'s sister, Elaine, also had one son working in the business, as a buyer in the purchasing department. He saw few opportunities for advancement in the company, since his relationship with his uncle—who determined promotions—was distant. Elaine and her children saw themselves as interested stockholders (her husband had died some years earlier) but had few opportunities to pursue a management career at the company.

In 1977 a tragedy engulfed the Brown family. John, Jr.'s wife, Helen, was kidnapped during a robbery attempt at their home and was murdered while the FBI and police were searching for her. This sent shock waves through the company and community, deeply affecting John, Jr., and his children. In the aftermath of his wife's death, John turned over much of the responsibility for operating the business to Reed Larson. With Larson in firm command (he was named president in 1978), the company continued to grow, reaching sales of over $100 milllion by 1980.

Under Larson, Brown workers began to sense that the company was becoming more impersonal, less like a family. The participative management philosophy was still preached but employees felt that it was rarely practiced. Dissatisfaction ran high. Turnover increased, and union organizing began in a company that had remained nonunion for almost 140 years. Coupled with this increasing dissatisfaction was the recession of the early 1980s. As sales began to drop, layoffs increased. Employment dropped from a high of 1,800 employees in 1979 to only 500 in 1983. Unemployment in the valley soared to over 15 percent, and the little community was economically devastated. The company continued to make a profit, but Larson began to feel pressure from stockholders, the board of directors, and the Brown family to turn the company around once again. This time, however, Larson offered his resignation. So now the company is at a critical juncture. John, Jr., who has remarried and developed some interests outside the business with his new wife, must find a replacement. He hoped his son Jim—or even Mike, if he were willing—would eventually run the business. But they do not have the experience of some of the more senior managers. John, Jr., has four options: (1) he can return to active involvement in the business and lead it until one of his sons is ready to take over; this will require him to give up some of his outside interests; (2) he can promote or bring in another president like Larson to run the business, but he will have to find someone who shares his management philosophy; also, this move might preclude his sons from ever taking over; (3) he can promote his son Jim (currently a division vice-president) to the presidency; however, Jim is still rather inexperienced and such a move might anger the veteran managers who feel they deserve a chance at the top spot; and (4) he can sell out; a number of firms have made offers. This final option would probably benefit the entire Brown family and stockholders financially, but the family would no longer be able to carry on the vision of John, Sr. The family's emotional attachment to the firm is something that John, Jr., feels very powerfully.

The Changing Nature of a Family Firm. This brief history of the Brown Corporation illustrates in several ways how the relationship of a family to the business it owns and manages will change over time. In the hectic early days of the firm's development, John, Sr., was concerned only with the survival of the business and made great sacrifices to achieve success. Later on, however, his concerns turned to keeping control of the business, spreading his personal philosophy of business to the employees, deciding whether or not to go public, and preparing his son to become the next president.

John, Jr., on the other hand, began his tenure as president by attempting to change his father's autocratic culture to a more democratic, participative management style. Along with the problem of changing the company culture, the second-generation president was faced with managing rapid growth and coordinating various subunits.

As the Brown Corporation entered the 1970s, John, Jr., became concerned with problems associated with bringing in professional managers whose values were quite different from his own. He also had to grapple with the problem of how to bring his children into the business and develop their talents. He and his older son were at odds over a number of issues, and this made planning for succession even more difficult. Finally, in the 1980s, the question of selling out is now confronting him.

We do not intend to suggest that all family firms move through all stages of the cycle in exactly the same way. The Brown Corporation illustrates the "typical" case, but there is some diversity in how a given family firm moves (or does not move) through these stages. In some of the firms we studied, the founder quickly moved through all four stages and eventually sold the business. In others, the family was totally concerned with sheer survival; growth, succession, and public ownership were not even issues. Still other family firms moved through the first two stages, developed a mature business, and never contemplated bringing in professional help. Their key problem was training family members for leadership and preparing for succession.

Thus we can see that family firms are a diverse group, with different concerns and different evolutionary patterns. However, there are some problems common to all, and these problems can be avoided and managed successfully if leaders of family firms understand the changes they will encounter as their businesses and families evolve.

Managing Change

Why do some family businesses succeed and others fail? The answer is frequently found in the interacting dynamics of business culture, family culture, and the culture of the governing board. By *culture* we mean the basic assumptions and values that underlie the behavior of the family and the firm (see Chapter Two for more on this concept). To a large extent this three-part cultural configuration—business, family, and board—determines whether or not the family business will continue to survive in succeeding generations.

Unfortunately, the cultures of most family businesses do not adapt well to a changing world. They stifle creativity and innovation, create unnecessary conflicts, and fail to prepare succeeding generations of leaders. However, certain kinds of cultural patterns in family firms do tend to create the conditions that help to ensure the firm's long-term survival.

The successful family firm is able to change its culture to adapt to the changing requirements of the business as it passes through the various developmental stages. One of the major purposes of the following chapters is to describe the kind of business, family, and board cultures that are needed if leaders of family firms are to manage continuity successfully and avoid the negative cycles and cultural patterns that most family firms find themselves in.

Forces in the business environment, in the legal system, and within the family and society are all combining to motivate those in family businesses to try new approaches to solve the problems they face. Traditional views of family businesses will undoubtedly change as we see major transformations in these businesses. Those family businesses that survive will have leaders who can anticipate such trends and can prepare their companies and families to adapt to a changing world.

Two

Understanding the Patterns of Business, Family, and Board Cultures

The behavior of the family firm is in large measure determined by the dynamics of cultures in the business, the family, and the firm's governing board. Understanding the configuration of these three cultures is the first step in managing successful transitions. Managers who have an accurate picture of the firm's cultural configuration have an opportunity to develop plans and change strategies based on a clear understanding of the total system. But more important, they can begin to *anticipate* problems. This allows the manager to plan for change well in advance, rather than waiting until it is too late. Unless the manager first understands the nature of family firm cultures, prudent action is impossible. Therefore the purpose of this chapter is to:

- Define the concept of culture and each of its four levels.
- Describe the three common cultures—business, family, and board—found in family firms.
- Discuss how the configuration of these three cultures changes over the life cycle of the family firm.

What Is Culture?

Up to this point, the term *culture* has been used rather loosely. In general, culture refers to the basic values and assumptions shared by a group. To understand the cultural configuration of a family firm, however, we need to be more specific.

The concept of culture as defined here can be applied to the business, the family, and the governing boards even though each of these systems is quite different in purpose and structure. The view of culture presented here is based on the work of a number of eminent anthropologists and more recently has been discussed by Edgar Schein (1981, 1984, 1985) and myself (Dyer, 1982, 1984a, 1984b). In this view, culture consists of four levels: artifacts, perspectives, values, and assumptions.

Artifacts. A newcomer in a foreign land is immediately struck by the sights, sounds, and smells that are different from his own culture. Similarly, someone entering a family business (or any organization) often hears and sees things that are beyond the ken of his own experience. We might call them the verbal, physical, and behavioral "artifacts" of that organization's culture, the overt expressions of the underlying belief system.

Verbal artifacts are the language and jargon used by members of an organization and the stories and myths they tell. Here are just a few examples.

The employees of one family business, a trucking company, refer to the firm's president as "the Supreme Intelligence"; they often circulate stories about him attempting to cheat them out of money that is rightfully theirs. A sarcastic company slogan is: "If the garbage collectors won't hire you, our company will." In the Brown Corporation, Reed Larson's nickname—"Jaws"— was a prominent verbal artifact. In addition, stories about Larson reprimanding or firing employees permeated the company culture.

Stories about family members were central to the culture of National Cash Register (NCR) in the early part of the twentieth century. John Patterson, NCR's founder, usually held a prominent place in these stories. Many of them are found in the memoirs of Stanley Allyn (1967, pp. 146–147), a close associate of Patterson:

> [Patterson's] actions often were capricious. Like many a genius in those days of greater rugged individualism, he governed by whim as well as by reason. His instincts were sound. He and his rela-

tives owned the business outright, and he could run
it as he pleased. Mr. Patterson was the master of
everyone's fate. He did not answer to stockholders,
unions, or government bodies for even his most
chimerical actions. . . . The NCR founder was in-
tolerant of careless work. Taking some of his friends
through the plant one day, he stopped before a cash
register and began to demonstrate its features. The
machine failed to work properly. He tried again,
with no better result. Without a word, the exasper-
ated industrialist picked up a sledge and demolished
the machine. "That is how we take care of faulty
merchandise," he said, as he walked away.

An organization's physical artifacts—the art, technology,
physical layout, accepted working attire, and so on—also play
a prominent role in creating the culture of a family firm. At
Bennett Enterprises, a Salt Lake City–based conglomerate, one
of the most celebrated physical artifacts is the heavy, black swing-
ing door that separates the office of president Michael Silva from
the rest of the organization. The door is commonly referred to
as "the Iron Curtain." Much like the "THINK" signs that
Thomas Watson placed in many of the IBM offices, the Iron
Curtain symbolically represents a key feature of Bennett's culture.
     Behavioral artifacts are also significant clues to under-
standing the cultures of family enterprises. At NCR, John Patterson would have his top executives arrive at work at 5:30 A.M.
and begin the day with calisthenics and horseback riding; he
was also quick to condemn anyone who indulged in alcohol or
tobacco. Patterson, who is described as being involved in every
facet of an employee's life, created at NCR one of the first corporate "welfare states." Such behaviors reflected Patterson's
beliefs about how to run an effective business.
     These are just a few examples of the kinds of artifacts
found in family firms. Artifacts are the starting point to understanding the culture, but they are just that—the starting point.
To understand the meanings behind these overt symbols, we
must probe deeper. We must discover why the president of the
trucking firm is nicknamed the "Supreme Intelligence" and why

Reed Larson is called "Jaws." What is the meaning of Michael Silva's "Iron Curtain," and why did John Patterson have his employees go horseback riding each morning? To answer these questions we must move to the next levels of culture.

Perspectives. The second level of culture consists of perspectives, "a coordinated set of ideas and actions a person uses in dealing with some problematic situation" (Becker, Geer, Hughes, and Strauss, 1961, p. 34). Thus perspectives encompass the socially shared rules and norms that are associated with the cultural artifacts and applicable in a given situation. Perspectives prescribe the bounds of acceptable behavior in specific situations.

To illustrate the use of perspectives in family firms, let us consider three common questions that members of family businesses often deem to be problematic. How do we train family members to be managers in our business? How do we handle disagreements? On what basis should we promote family members?

Perspectives on these issues vary greatly. Regarding training, for example, some family firms such as Neiman-Marcus believe that family members can be successful only by working their way up the ranks. In contrast, one family-owned hotel chain uses a mentoring system—putting family members in key positions and then providing technical or managerial support to help them. Others solve this problem by sending family members to work in other organizations to receive their "management training."

Different perspectives are also employed when families face dissent and disagreements. The leader of one Latin American conglomerate brings his wife and children together for a family "powwow"; he frequently includes outside consultants as mediators. Other families, such as the Du Ponts, have engaged in highly emotional disagreements. Their modus operandi for handling disputes has been to resort to litigation, which has brought bitter division within the family. Still other families manage conflict by avoiding it. They will design rather ingenious organizational structures that allow family members to work independently of one another and thus avoid interaction, or they will divide the ownership and management of the company to allow family members to run their operations separately.

We also find a variety of perspectives regarding promotions. Some firms allow only family members to lead the business. In the early years of Procter & Gamble, family membership was the major criterion for advancement (although this changed when there were no family members willing and able to run the company). Bennett Enterprises rewards people based on the president's bottom-line definition of performance. Other family businesses take a middle-ground approach to promotion. Performance is always important, but family members are given preference if two candidates appear to be equal. The Brown Corporation is an example of a company that holds such a view.

Values. Inextricably connected with perspectives are the shared values of the family, company employees, and members of the board of directors. Perspectives define specific courses of action in particular situations. Values are broader, transsituational principles that serve as guides for overall behavior. Values reflect general goals, ideals, and standards, such as ''serve the customer,'' ''promote from within,'' and ''show initiative.'' These values are often articulated in statements of organizational identity or management philosophy.

Many of the companies in our study had developed a formal statement of their philosophy—which generally reflected the views held by the company's founder. Some, like John Patterson, went to great lengths to develop and inculcate their basic beliefs upon their employees. Patterson created a list of eighty-two reasons why NCR was a good place to work and established what might be called a ''propaganda department'' to disseminate his ideas throughout the organization. He also developed a primer of his philosophy that was required reading for all employees attending the company training school.

This is not to say that all values are found in formal statements of management philosophy. Many times the values are informal in nature, recognized by participants in the culture but not written down. Moreover, we often find that members of an organization fail to follow prescribed values and may even contradict them. Thus we must be careful to distinguish between the ''ideal'' and the ''real'' values.

Assumptions. The previous three levels of culture have moved from highly ''tangible'' artifacts to more abstract values.

At the innermost core of a group's culture, however, are the very basic assumptions that form the foundation of the culture. While they may use different terminology to describe them, scholars refer to these tacit assumptions as the core beliefs that underpin overt artifacts, perspectives, and values (Kluckhohn, 1951; Kluckhohn and Strodtbeck, 1961; Bem, 1970; Rokeach, 1973; Homans, 1950; Light, 1979).

To illustrate, let us look in on a remarkable annual ritual of Levi Strauss & Co. For generations, the annual reports were closely guarded family secrets. To meet the legal requirement that each shareholder see an annual report, every year David Beronio, a trusted family adviser, had just one copy typed up. At the shareholders' meeting, he personally carried it around the room, showing it to each stockholder. Junior executives and minor shareholders got only a brief glance at the balance sheet before it disappeared into Beronio's locked drawer. As the board expanded and the fiscal problems multiplied, the number of copies increased. But each copy was assigned a number, and each one was carefully collected at the end of the annual meeting (Cray, 1978, p. 185).

The behavior itself is a cultural artifact. It identifies a perspective: that only family members have the prerogative to scrutinize the company's annual reports; nonfamily members were given just enough information to meet the requirements of the law. If we add to this certain other perspectives indicating a desire to avoid any actions that would expose the family to public scrutiny, then a broader value becomes apparent: that secrecy about company and family affairs is important. Based on these data, we can infer that this behavioral artifact, its accompanying perspectives, and its values appear to reflect a basic assumption: those outside the family should not be trusted.

Categories of Basic Assumptions. Although there may be many "types" of basic assumptions underlying the culture of a family firm, the works of a number of social scientists (for example, Kluckhohn and Strodtbeck, 1961; Parsons and Shils, 1951; Bem, 1970; Schein, 1981, 1985) and our own studies have indicated that there are seven categories particularly useful in deciphering the cultural patterns of family firms. These categories are listed here, along with descriptions of various orientations that might be found in the three "systems" of the family firm. These categories illustrate how a group's assumptions about themselves, others, and the world in which they live differ greatly from one another and create very different kinds of cultures. (For a more detailed explanation of each of these categories, see the appendix.)

1. *Assumptions about relationships.* Are relationships between members of the organization primarily lineal (that is, hierarchical), collateral (group-oriented), or individualistic?
2. *Assumptions about human nature.* Are humans basically good, basically evil, or neutral (neither good nor evil)?
3. *Assumptions about the nature of truth.* Is "truth" (that is, correct decisions) discovered from external authority figures, or is it determined by a process of personal investigation and testing?
4. *Assumptions about the environment.* Can humans master the environment, must they be subjugated by it, or should they attempt to harmonize with it?
5. *Assumptions about universalism.* Should all members of the organization be evaluated by the same standards, or should certain individuals be given preferential treatment?
6. *Assumptions about time.* Are members of the organization primarily oriented to the past, the present, or the future?
7. *Assumptions about the nature of human activity.* Are humans basically active (a "doing" orientation)? Are they passive, unable to alter existing circumstances (a "being" orientation)? Or do they have as a primary goal the development of self as an integrated whole (a "being-in-becoming" orientation)?

Cultural Patterns. In any business, family, or governing board, a set of tacit assumptions forms the core of the culture. This set of assumptions, and their interrelationships, form what is called the cultural pattern. It is this pattern that is important to uncover. In one company, the GEM Corporation (fictional name), the culture was founded on the following assumptions:

1. Relationships were assumed to be collateral (group-oriented) in nature, much like siblings in a large family.

2. Fellow employees were deemed to be basically good and capable of governing themselves.
3. Truth and knowledge were to be gained through conflict, confrontation, and the testing of new ideas. No one was assumed to have all the answers.

This particular pattern of assumptions created a culture that valued autonomy and individual initiative in a combative climate while simultaneously fostering support through strong kinship ties. Much like siblings, GEM managers would "fight" with one another to get at the "truth" and make the best decisions. The sense of family and belonging (the company followed a policy of lifetime employment) allowed employees to confront one another in a highly supportive atmosphere.

In contrast, some companies foster relationships that are hierarchically ordered rather than collateral. People are asssumed to be untrustworthy, and knowledge is to be found in the company's rules and regulations rather than discovered through conflict. People in such organizations often conform carefully to company policy and strictly follow orders from those in authority.

In summary, the key to the culture of the family firm lies in the pattern of the core assumptions of the business, the family, and the governing board.

Common Cultural Configurations

As we discussed in Chapter One, the cultural configuration of a particular company is significant because it forms the basis for understanding the complexities of that firm as it evolves over its life cycle; the leader's understanding (or lack of it) will help or hinder the firm's ability to survive. The possible configurations of the business, family, and board cultures are presented in Figure 1.

The nature and purpose of a business enterprise, a family, and a governing body that meets infrequently are obviously quite different. As the various cultural patterns in these groups are described in this chapter, the reader will notice the differences in their purpose and function. To that end, we have included rather detailed descriptions of some family firms that exemplify each pattern.

Figure 1. Cultural Configuration of a Family Firm.

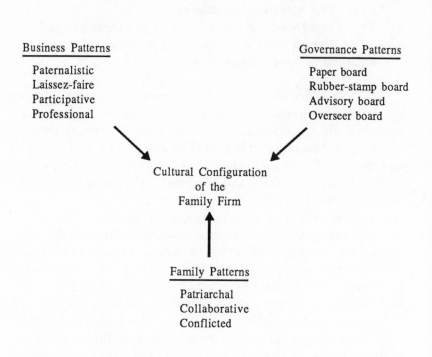

Business Patterns   Governance Patterns

Paternalistic   Paper board
Laissez-faire   Rubber-stamp board
Participative   Advisory board
Professional   Overseer board

Cultural Configuration
of the
Family Firm

Family Patterns

Patriarchal
Collaborative
Conflicted

Cultural Patterns in the Business

Four cultural patterns commonly found in the business, and the basic assumptions of each along the seven cultural dimensions, are presented in Table 1. These four patterns represent the general types found in the business side of a family firm. There are, of course, exceptions and variations. Still, these types provide a point of reference, a means of comparing the cultural patterns of these firms.

The basic assumptions underlying these patterns reflect vastly different means of controlling members of the organization. The paternalistic pattern, for example, is founded on assumptions that emphasize the personal power and charisma of founders and their families; this gives them the means to perpetuate family domination of the firm. The professional pattern, on the other hand, emphasizes impersonal rules and

Table 1. Cultural Patterns of the Family Business.

Category of Assumptions	Paternalistic	Laissez Faire	Participative	Professional
Relationships	Lineal (hierarchical)	Lineal	Collateral (group-oriented)	Individualistic
Human nature	People are basically untrustworthy	People are "good" and trustworthy	People are good and trustworthy	People neither good nor evil—neutral stance
Nature of truth	Truth resides in the founder/family	Truth resides in founder/family, although "outsiders" given autonomy	Truth found in group decision making/participation	Truth found in professional rules of conduct
The environment	Proactive stance	Harmonizing/proactive stance	Harmonizing/proactive stance	Reactive/proactive stance
Universalism	Particularistic (nepotism)	Particularistic	Universalistic	Universalistic
Time	Present- or past-oriented	Present- or past-oriented	Present- or future-oriented	Present-oriented
Human activity	Doing orientation	Doing orientation	Being-in-becoming orientation	Doing orientation

"professional" conduct as the means of control. Each cultural pattern, in its own way, describes a configuration of assumptions that leads to different forms of control.

The Paternalistic Culture. In the paternalistic culture, the most common pattern, relationships are arranged hierarchically, with the founder or other family leaders retaining all decision-making authority and the key information about the firm's operations. Family members are given preference over nonfamily employees. There is a high distrust of "outsiders," and the founder and family closely supervise their employees, who are given little discretion in performing their tasks. Employees are assumed to have a proactive, "doing" orientation in carrying out the wishes of the owning family. The firm's environment orientation generally tends to be proactive in developing new products or markets; however, a few paternalistic firms tend to create a particular market niche and stay within it. They will "harmonize" with the surrounding environment, setting up a variety of barriers to market entry or creating other competitive advantages as a means of protecting their markets. The paternalistic firms also seem to have one of two "time" orientations. Some are clearly oriented to the past: carrying on the founder's and family's legacy is their primary aim, and the entire cultural mosaic is steeped in family traditions. However, some paternalistic firms are very present-oriented. Although often maintaining some traditions, the leaders of these enterprises quickly change to meet new threats and challenges. Tradition is less important than remaining profitable in the short run.

One company that illustrates this paternalistic cultural pattern is the Western Freight Company (fictional name), a small freight company firm that currently operates in thirty-five states (Buckner, 1985). The company was acquired by Hal Pearson in the early 1970s and is owned by himself, his wife, and another family that provided some of the original capital. Pearson keeps a relatively small staff—five managers and nine clerical workers. He has twenty-five drivers and a few part-time dock workers although this number varies with the work load.

Pearson, at age sixty-five, appears to be in relatively good health and is determined to run his company "forever." He refuses to delegate much authority, if any; the entire staff reports directly to him. The office layout also reinforces the centrality of his position. Pearson's office is in the center, surrounded by all the staff offices, and he leaves both doors of his office open so he can monitor all the company's activities. Pearson's wife has handled most of the "book work," and his daughter acts as secretary/receptionist and maintains the accounts for interstate operations.

Pearson has tried to maintain a "family" feeling in his organization. Birthdays and holidays are celebrated at the office, and Pearson has been known to treat his employees to lunch. He has helped employees who faced some problem at home. One of the more common rituals occurs when there is a surplus shipment of candy bars: Pearson ostentatiously walks through all the offices distributing the candy like Santa Claus.

Although employees like certain aspects of this paternalism, many see Pearson as quite condescending. One supervisor of the drivers, who is fifty-five years old, says that Pearson treats him like one of the kids. Employees also complain that Pearson never listens to their ideas. One employee said, "Mr. Pearson doesn't even listen. You make a suggestion to him and he'll tell you it's ridiculous. They you'll go in the next day and he'll tell you about the same idea and tell you how wonderful it is. He won't do anything unless it's his idea." Such behavior has earned Pearson the nickname "the Supreme Intelligence." Pearson's style of giving out compliments and rewards also reinforces this image. He rewards family and favored employees rather capriciously. His daughter was given the most expensive typewriter in the company, which created widespread resentment. Pearson also has the reputation for left-handed compliments such as "You may be stupid but you do your job well."

Pearson is also said to distrust most employees. He closely monitors all drivers' fuel purchases and their mileage. One staff member commented, "You're okay as long as he doesn't think you're a thief. As soon as he gets it into his head that you've stolen one gallon or one mile or one anything, you're through. The simple fact is that people who are dishonest expect everyone else to be dishonest" (Buckner, 1985, p.3). Such behavior has greatly affected the morale and self-esteem of employees to the point that the informal company slogan is "If the garbage collectors won't hire you, Western will."

In 1984 the company experienced the loss of several key people, primarily because of their inability to cope with the paternalistic culture. Few have been replaced—Pearson has taken over many of their duties himself. "There is no comparison between the way things were run in the past [before the key managers left] and the way I'm running things now," he commented. "Business is going much much better" (p. 6). Later that same year Pearson's daughter also quit in a dispute with the company claims clerk. She had given her father an ultimatum: either fire the claims clerk or she would quit. Pearson refused to give in to his daughter's demands, and she left the business. Now Pearson has no family successor available and has devoted little time to thinking about the future or succession planning.

Western Freight Company clearly has a number of problems idiosyncratic to this one firm. Still, it highlights key features of the paternalistic cultural pattern: dominance by founder and family, and close control of employees.

The Laissez-Faire Culture. The laissez-faire cultural pattern is similar to the paternalistic pattern in many ways. Relationships are again hierarchical in nature and family members are given favored positions. Members of the organization are expected to be proactive in achieving the goals of the family. These organizations have similar stances toward the environment and toward time. They differ, however, in two dimensions: human nature and truth. The laissez-faire culture is based on high levels of trust between the workers and the family. The founder and family delegate a great deal of authority to lower-level decision makers. Here, too, "truth" about the firm's ultimate mission and goals resides in the founder and the family, but they give employees wide latitude in achieving them. Thus, while the founder and family determine the ends, the employees are given the power to determine many of the means. In the paternalistic firm, the family specifies both the ends and the means.

One family firm that has adopted the laissez-faire pattern in the past is Levi Strauss & Co. (Cray, 1978; Dyer, 1984a).

The company was founded in 1886 by Levi Strauss, a Jewish immigrant from Bavaria who began in New York as an itinerant peddler selling the wares of his older brothers. He eventually moved to San Francisco and established a store that sold domestic and foreign dry goods, clothing, and household furnishings. In addition to Levi, there were four partners in the business: his sisters, Fanny and Mary, and his brothers, Jonas and Louis.

Every day, Levi left home at 9:00 A.M. and walked to work, arriving some time around 10:00. A trusted employee, Philip Fisher, would open and close the store. He routinely checked the sales figures for the previous day and then spent the rest of the day chatting with employees and customers. Employees, who called the boss ''Levi,'' were able to look forward to lifetime employment. The Strauss family and their descendants were known for helping employees during times of trouble. They paid the medical bills of one employee when he became ill with diphtheria and gave him $1,000 to cover his debts (he eventually became plant manager).

The story of how Levi Strauss got into the denim pants business is rather curious. During the late 1860s a tailor named Jacob Davis invented riveted denim pants—quite by accident. He was making denim pants for a silver miner in Nevada when he ran out of thread. He noticed some rivets lying on the table and decided to use them instead of thread to fasten the pockets. They were an instant success, for the riveted pockets did not rip out. Orders for the riveted jeans began to increase and Davis was able to build a rather lucrative business. However, Davis was fearful that his competitors would copy his idea. Because he lacked the $68 for the patent fee, he wrote Levi Strauss in 1871, offering 50 percent of any profits if Levi would pay the patent fee. Strauss accepted. In 1873 Levi established a plant to manufacture the new pants, giving Jacob Davis complete authority over production. The plant employed sixty women, who worked on a piece-rate system.

In 1874, David Stern, Fanny Strauss's husband, died. A few years later her sister, Mary, also died. Shortly thereafter, Mary's husband, William Sahlein, married Fanny; therefore two-fifths of the partnership rested in the Stern/Sahlein family, which allowed Fanny to bolster the careers of her four sons; eventually they took over the business.

After Levi Strauss's death, the Stern brothers followed his laissez-faire tradition. They routinely deferred all major manufacturing decisions to Jacob Davis, and relied on Philip Fisher and his assistant, Albert Hershfield, for financial advice. The Sterns were characterized as "absentee owners" although Jacob Stern, the oldest, did attempt to carry on Levi Strauss's values. In 1918, company profits were only $45,000 on a $1.6 million investment. The Sterns thought about selling the business, because they lacked a clear successor. However, one brother, Sigmund Stern, found a son-in-law, Walter Haas, who was interested in joining the business. In 1919, Haas, a graduate of the University of California, was brought in to be groomed for the presidency.

Haas soon discovered that the salesmen were rather lackadaisical and needed more supervision. He also saw a need to update their accounting and bookkeeping systems and to develop a system to assess employee potential and assign jobs based on qualifications. Thus, new systems were designed to improve productivity and efficiency. Although these new artifacts represented cultural change in the company at one level, they were consistent with the prevailing cultural pattern and did not reflect a deeper change in the core assumptions of the culture. The company continued to promote lifetime employment by creating make-work jobs for older employees. The family also continued to allow employees a great deal of autonomy.

In 1922, Walter Haas convinced his brother-in-law, Dan Koshland, to help him manage the business. Koshland, a banker, seemed to complement Haas well. The two men began to shuffle personnel, prod salesmen to sell more, and tighten financial controls (Cray, 1978). In 1925 the company began to give bonuses to women factory workers (before that time they had only been given to managers). The Stern brothers died in the 1920s; Walter Haas and Dan Koshland not only managed the company but were the principal stockholders as well.

Events during the Depression of the 1930s underscored the family's commitment to their beliefs. Sales slumped dramatically, but no one was fired or laid off. The company sold some items at a loss, just to keep people working. The family could have closed the plant, but Haas and Koshland were backed by the family fortune and family pride. Employees worked three days a week, took pay cuts, and did some work sharing. For a period of time in 1932, manufacturing was shut down, but employees were kept working by refurbishing the plant. Finally, in 1933 Levi Strauss returned to full employment and wages were increased by fifty percent. Such a display of cooperation and trust between workers and management reflected the core assumptions of the culture. This tradition was continued by Walter Haas, Jr., and Peter Haas (the fourth generation) until certain events in the early 1970s changed the company culture.

The example of Levi Strauss & Co. suggests an alternative to the paternalistic pattern. While maintaining control of overall objectives, the founder and the family can foster a more laissez-faire culture based on trust and can delegate much of their authority to nonfamily members.

The Participative Culture. The participative culture is relatively rare; we found only four instances in our panel. The participative pattern is based on assumptions that vary dramatically from the paternalistic and laissez-faire cultures. Relationships tend to be more collateral in nature, more group-oriented. The status and power of the family are minimized, to create a more egalitarian atmosphere in the firm. This is not to say that the founder and family are on equal footing with nonfamily members, but this kind of pattern discounts family membership and ownership as the primary basis for power and influence. Relationships are based on high levels of trust. Members of the organization are often obsessed with developing and maintaining trusting relationships. Co-workers are deemed to be basically good and trustworthy, so close supervision or other overt control mechanisms are avoided.

In contrast to the previous two patterns, which emphasized the founder or family as the repository of information about the operation of the business, the participative pattern emphasizes using the group to make decisions. All employees are considered potential resources to solve problems and provide valuable information. The environmental orientations tend to be rather proactive; these firms take significant steps to "manage" their environments. They are often oriented to both the present and the future, focusing on the "here and now" problems as well as doing significant amounts of future planning. Nepotism and other forms of favoritism are formally disdained. Evaluation criteria are applied universally, and overall performance and contribution to the group are often the salient criteria. Finally, the participative culture has a "being-in-becoming" orientation toward the nature of human activity. Personal growth and development of individual employees are seen as an integral part of the work of the organization. "Doing" is not enough. It must be done the "right" way, allowing for widest participation, thus giving members of the organization the opportunity to magnify their talents. In such a culture it is not uncommon to hear top management comment that the key to success is the personal growth and development of the employees.

One organization that has been known to exhibit this type of cultural pattern is the Donnelly Corporation. The company was founded in 1905 by Bernard Donnelly, who created an organization to provide the furniture industry (and later the automobile industry) with high-quality mirrors. He ran the company according to traditional business practices of the time. However, his son, John Donnelly, who took over the business when Bernard died, developed a different approach. With the help of an outside consultant, Carl Frost, John Donnelly established a "Scanlon" philosophy of management. The Scanlon plan at Donnelly involved establishing group bonuses, creating work teams, and doing away with control mechanisms such as time clocks.

During the late 1960s John Donnelly was also influenced by the writings of Mary Parker Follett and became intensely involved in the growing field of organization development (OD). With the help of his top-management team, which included Bob Doyle, an OD specialist, the company began to adopt many of the ideas from prominent OD practitioners. The company developed a relationship with Rensis Likert in the early 1960s, who was then at the Institute for Social Research at the University of Michigan. Likert had just developed his System 4 model of leadership, which is based on the assumption that participation of workers in decision making leads to both better decisions and highly committed employees. Likert extensively surveyed company employees to assess their management styles. Based on the survey data, the Donnelly Corporation hired Robert Blake to do "grid training" that encouraged managers to be more participative. With this emphasis on participation, Donnelly's leadership attempted to create a more egalitarian, group-oriented culture where status symbols would be disdained.

In the 1970s, John Donnelly became chairman of the board, and, for the first time, a nonfamily manager was named the new president. In the late 1970s, the company was in the throes of a major recession. To cope with the recession, top management began a series of moves that were clearly seen as nonparticipative: They ordered pay cuts, delayed raises, and declared plant shutdowns. As a result of these actions, the participative culture of Donnelly was threatened. Thus, John Donnelly felt it was necessary to take corrective action. A new chief executive officer was appointed, signalling a return to the participative culture of the past. This return was illustrated by the way the company handled the problem of a shrinking market in the early 1980s. The company had to reduce overhead by $1 million in 1981. Workers were allowed to participate fully in deciding how to make these cuts. More than forty employees were transferred to other departments, took lower-paying jobs in the company, or left the company through a joint decision-making process. Even those who left the company generally had positive feelings—they understood the reasons for the decisions and felt that they had an opportunity to express their views. One Donnelly employee said that these cuts could only have been made in this way because the culture emphasized trust and cooperation among employees when faced with a problem.

The participative culture at Donnelly was created by a leader interested in worker participation and shaped by consultants and company employees who had been exposed to and believed in participative management. The assumptions of this cultural pattern are clearly at odds with the other two patterns, and have different outcomes, as we will see in future chapters.

The Professional Culture. By "professional culture," I do
not mean a culture that is more professional than another. This
term is used to describe the kind of cultural pattern that often
emerges when professional managers assume the management
of a family business. Of course a founder could also create this
kind of cultural pattern, and not all professional managers adhere
to this kind of philosophy, but by and large certain professional
management codes of conduct often accompany these managers
as they enter a family firm.

In contrast to the paternalistic, laissez-faire, and participative cultural patterns, which emphasize either hierarchical or
collateral relationships, the professional culture is based on the
assumption that individual motivation and achievement should
be paramount. Professional cultures are often highly competitive,
with managers striving to reach the top positions. For those who
achieve within this system, individual rewards are enormous.
The orientation toward human nature is often neutral; employees
are seen as being neither necessarily good nor evil but, rather,
motivated by rewards or punishment. In firms with this pattern,
we often found reward and control systems that were situation-
specific; in some situations employees seemed to be trusted, in
other cases there appeared to be a great deal of distrust. There
also appeared to be a similar contingency approach to gathering
information and making decisions. Whereas task forces, management committees, and the like were often used to make decisions,
in other cases managers would rely solely on decision models
and principles obtained from their schooling or professional experience. However, the criteria for making decisions was generally clear—maximizing one's own rewards using a return-on-
investment logic.

The professional managers that we studied often found
themselves in situations where they were called on to turn around
a faltering family business, so they often found themselves in a
"reactor mode," responding to environmental forces and being forced to "put out the many fires" that were threatening
to consume the firm. Others were highly proactive in attempting
to increase the firm's profitability and often engaged in long-
range or strategic planning; they were future oriented. The

professionals had a clear "doing" orientation. Getting the job done—and this generally meant bottom-line results—was crucial. *How* the job got done was relatively unimportant. Such a passion for results leads to receiving rewards based on demonstrated skills or performance. Thus the criteria for advancement—at least publicly—was universal, although in some of the firms we studied, political intrigue and "connections" were used informally to gain rewards.

The professional culture is illustrated by International Harvester during the presidency of Archie R. McCardell. International Harvester was founded in the mid-1800s by Cyrus McCormick, who invented the reaper in Virginia. McCormick moved the company headquarters to Chicago to supply midwestern farmers with farm equipment. From the beginning, the company culture was paternalistic, with family members being closely associated with the business. The company offered lifetime employment to anyone lucky enough to get a job there. The company prospered and by 1950 had reached 90,000 employees.

But during the early 1970s the company faltered badly. President Brooks McCormick, great-grandnephew of Cyrus, commissioned a number of consulting firms to study the firm's problems. One of them, Booz Allen & Hamilton, recommended that an outside professional manager be brought in to overhaul the company. Brooks McCormick consented. In 1977, Archie McCardell, then president and chief operating officer of Xerox Corporation, was chosen for the job. His financial incentives were almost beyond belief: a $460,000 base salary, a $1.5 million bonus up front, and a $1.8 million loan at 6 percent interest to buy International Harvester stock. Thus his incentives to succeed were great. McCardell said that he took the job for three reasons: "More money, the immediate chance to run a multi-billion dollar corporation, and the challenge of improving the performance of one of the stodgiest companies in the industry" ("McCardell Starts Things Moving . . . ," p. 28).

McCardell began his tenure by immediately rejecting the budgets of the group presidents because they failed to meet his standards of careful business analysis. This had never been done before, and it certainly shook things up. McCardell also began a series of cost-cutting programs in manufacturing, product design, purchasing, and personnel. Employees were laid off and fired in order to meet the new cost objectives. However, McCardell brought in a number of new managers who resonated to his cost-cutting programs. He took steps to bolster the finance department and increase captial investment. He restructured the management committees to improve efficiency and eliminated some meetings that he felt were a waste of time. McCardell rewarded his favorite managers generously with bonuses and a variety of perks. He would play subordinates off against one another to encourage competition as well as compliance with his wishes.

While McCardell had indeed transformed the culture of the corporate staff, his cost-cutting programs were greeted with antipathy by the union. McCardell entered contract negotiations in 1979 with a list of demands that were unacceptable to the union. McCardell was unwavering, and a long and bitter strike ensued. It lasted over five months and was extremely costly; the company lost $225 million in the first fiscal quarter alone. McCardell never recovered. Although he contined to attempt to consolidate operations, sell off unprofitable parts of the business, and cut costs, the company suffered a staggering loss in 1981—$767.3 million. The board of directors ousted McCardell in May 1982, then announced the next day that the union had approved concessions that would save the company several hundred million dollars.

Although much more could be said about International Harvester and McCardell's impact, what is clear is that McCardell attempted to create a cultural pattern that was, in many ways, antithetical to the paternalistic culture the McCormick family had embraced. McCardell emphasized and rewarded individual achievement and bottom-line results. His business acumen and professional training led him to take steps that he felt were necessary for the efficient operation of the business. Despite his best attempts, however, he was undone by his underestimation of the power of the union (Harvard case no. 9–381–053).

Cultural Patterns in the Family

The cultures of the families that owned and managed the businesses we studied varied greatly. The number and ages of family members, deaths and divorces, the family's history of managing crises and solving problems all combined to influence the cultural patterns. Other writers, such as Rosenblatt, de Mik, Anderson, and Johnson (1985), Kepner (1983), and Levinson (1983), have noted some of the features of the families involved in a family business. Our research in many ways complements theirs, for we found similar patterns. We discovered three common cultural patterns in families connected with a family business; each represents different ways of handling authority, achieving goals, making decisions, and managing conflict.

The Patriarchal (Matriarchal) Family. In the patriarchal family, the father (or other family leader, perhaps the mother or one of the children) is the dominant authority figure. Family life revolves around him and his desires. All major decisions about the family are made by the family leader and family members are expected to follow obediently. The spouse and children play a subservient role and are largely dependent on the leader for guidance. The family leader sets the goals for all the family. Leaders are often very secretive about their activities, rarely taking their children and at times even their spouses into their confidence. They have little confidence in the family's ability to handle more responsibility and information.

Such traditional patterns were found in families such as that of John Brown, Sr., in the Brown Corporation and John Patterson at NCR. These patterns were particularly common in the Latin American and European companies that we studied; the heads of these families were the undisputed authority figures and generally dominated family life until their deaths.

The Collaborative Family. Unlike the traditional leaders, the heads of collaborative families often take their spouses and children into their confidence and rely on them for information and ideas when making decisions. Each family member has the opportunity to exert some power. The family creates and shares goals and values, and places a high priority on maintaining family solidarity. Family members see the interdependencies in their relationships and make every effort to work cooperatively.

The Delta Corporation (fictional name) was owned by a family that had developed a collaborative culture. The founder, while still the dominant authority figure, frequently consulted with his wife and children when making decisions. When the time came to think about succession planning, he included his wife and his children in the process. In meetings attended by his wife, his children, and at times nonfamily executives and consultants, the founder candidly explored the problems and dilemmas he was facing. Painful issues—death, retirement, estate planning, choosing a successor—were discussed and debated. The family's overall reaction to using such a process was highly favorable. They found that collaborating on these kinds of problems led to increased understanding within the family and increased family solidarity to solve its problems.

The Conflicted Family. The conflicted family is characterized by an absence of shared goals. Individual motives and desires guide everyone's actions. Family members tend to mistrust one another and seem to be constantly "protecting" themselves against the designs of others. Relationships are counterdependent in nature, always in conflict. These families are often unable to develop problem-solving mechanisms to resolve their differences. Thus they tend to rely on lawsuits, or they merely avoid one another. These families are characterized by mistrust, conflict, and alienation.

We found numerous examples of families that fell into this pattern. One of the more sensational cases is the Du Pont family, who typically "solved" their succession problems by either never speaking to one another again or by filing a lawsuit (Chandler and Salisbury, 1971). Similar conflicts between the sons of Walter Boss, the owner of A. T. Cross Co., almost destroyed the company. Their ownership dispute was eventually resolved by the Rhode Island Supreme Court (Cook, 1976, p. 32).

One of the more visible examples of such conflicts was the feud in the early 1970s between Frank Jarman and his father, Maxey, at Genesco Inc., one of the world's largest apparel companies. Carruth (1975, p. 111) describes some of the differences between the two men: "The elder Jarman [Maxey] is something of an egghead; he reads as many as twenty books concurrently and collects abstract paintings. He does not smoke or drink, and he avoids physical exercise of any kind. A devout Southern Baptist, Jarman rereads the Bible every year and says simply, 'Religion is the center of my life.' Son Frank never goes to church, eschews the Bible, and talks about the 'hypocrisy' of the devout. Married and divorced twice, he has no children, and is very much a man's man. A friend of both men says flatly, 'Maxey reads more books in a month than Frank ever has.' The younger Jarman is an athletic person, who rises at 5:30 A.M. to jog two miles before the workday begins."

Obviously there are marked differences in the personalities of the two men. Furthermore, their business philosophies often collided, and they frequently criticized one another publicly. Frank revealed that he and his father "never had any private, personal discussions about the business—only professional ones"; Maxey confessed that he "really doesn't know his own son" (p. 111). These differences led to constant skirmishes between father and son, until Frank finally ousted Maxey in a 1973 board meeting. After these battles and Maxey's retirement, the two did not speak except for a few public appearances.

In summary, the three family patterns reflect different assumptions about family relationships, the basic nature of other family members, and the method of solving problems and resolving conflicts. These cultural patterns are often the source of many of the frustrations and problems that plague family businesses.

Cultural Patterns in Governing Boards

One of the most difficult groups to study in a family business is often the company's board of directors. Meetings are held only a few times a year, and outsiders know little about the inner workings of these groups. Much of the data we were able to gather on the functioning of the governing boards was based on interviews with board members; in some cases we were given access to meeting minutes. Thus the picture of what actually occurs during board meetings is somewhat incomplete, for we were unable to observe the behavior firsthand. Still, we were able to obtain an overall sense of the structure and function of these boards. We discovered that the assumptions about the role of the board of directors varied from firm to firm, and we defined four basic roles.

The Paper Board. "Paper" boards have a few board members—generally family members—listed "on paper" to meet the requirements of the law, but they perform little function. Because the founder and his family make all the decisions anyway, the board meetings are considered redundant, a review of decisions already made. Board meetings are held irregularly, if at all, and then are carried out in a perfunctory fashion.

A good example of a paper board is found in the Brown Corporation where the board consisted of John Brown, Sr., his wife, and John Brown, Jr. John, Jr., describes how the board functioned when he was elected company president (Dyer, 1984a, p. 73):

> [When] my father and mother came back from Florida, I used to pick them up at the airport and bring them home. [One time when I picked them up] it was late in the day so they had dinner at our house. So over a cocktail my father said: "I think you ought to be president since you are doing it all." I said, "no." He said, "what do you mean, no!" I said, "well, there are two reasons: one is that I don't know enough about the job to do it right, and number two, all you are going to do is give me a title and not the authority." That took a little while to discuss. Anyway, he stayed the summer and then went back to Florida, and . . . the same thing happened the next year. The following year, however, he came back and said, "I'm sorry you missed the Board meeting." And I said, "when was it?" And he said, "this morning." . . . I said, "well, what happened?" He said, "congratulations, you have been elected president." So that is how I became president.

The Rubber-Stamp Board. The rubber-stamp board is a formally organized board that often includes members outside the family, generally friends—the family banker, the family lawyer, the family accountant—who can provide advice as well as connections to the broader business community. Their role is to support the decisions of the founder and the family, since they have little power to change the family's favored policies.

The Advisory Board. Although the family still controls the advisory board, outside directors have some influence on decisions. Outside board members are often seen as protecting the interests of company shareholders—particularly the interests of nonfamily members—and can often render invaluable advice to a family business. After going public, the Brown Corporation set up an advising board, which played a crucial role in mediating family conflicts. John, Jr., describes how one outside board member diffused a potentially damaging conflict (Dyer, 1984a, p. 5):

> We were in a little downturn, and so my father wanted me to fire [one of my most trusted managers] Tom Nelson. I said, "what for? The guy is producing tremendously." Well, he argued with me. . . . He said, "this has got to come before the Board." I said, "that is dumb—don't get outsiders mixed up in a family argument." So we went to the Board meeting—my father was the Chairman. He did call the meeting to order, but he never even asked for approval of the previous minutes. He said, "we are going to discuss Thomas Nelson." There were three outside Board members. . . . He told his story and turned to me and said, "have you got anything to say?" I said, "yes I do" and so I gave my story. The facts all said keep this guy. My father's emotions said to get rid of him. There was no other discussion and my father said, "are you ready to vote?" Well, I argued about that, I didn't want to vote, but he called for a vote. The vote was five to get rid of him and two abstentions—Bill Johnson and I did not vote. . . . I can't tell you a thing that

happened the rest of the Board meeting because
I was mad and I sat there figuring out what I was
going to do. I didn't really like going somewhere
else to look for a job, but that was where I was.
Immediately after the meeting was over, a [board
member] who was president of one of the banks
who had been a long-time friend of both my father and I said, ''I have got to talk to you right
now.'' . . . He said, ''I suspect you wonder why
the three of us [meaning the outsiders] voted the
way we did. . . . Well, I will tell you. . . . I have
been involved with family organizations all my
business life and I have saved an awful lot of
them. . . . There is no one man that is all so important to the company. You can find another
guy that is just as good as Nelson or better. But
if we had voted with you, your father would have
never gotten over it. It would have split this company right down the middle. Now, with you, you
are young enough to get over it and I suggest you
start right now.'' I had to go home and think about
that. I went to work the next morning.

The Overseer Board. The overseer board meets regularly
and may, during crisis periods, run the day-to-day affairs of
the company. This board not only elects officers but makes
the major decisions on strategy and policy. Outside interests—
often venture capitalists—who want to protect their investment scrutinize carefully the affairs of the business and will
frequently intervene to stop any actions they feel are unwar-
ranted. Overseer boards are found in those family firms that
have gone public, for which the family no longer controls the
majority of shares. Outside board members may operate from
a very strong power base, especially if they can demonstrate
to shareholders that family actions have adversely affected the
stock price. Overseer boards are arenas for high conflict, since
the goals of the outside investors and the family are often quite
different.

Cultural Configurations and
the Family Firm Life Cycle

Having described the four cultural patterns of the business, three family patterns, and four patterns in the governing boards, we can now begin to examine the many possible combinations of these three entities. We have called these combinations the "cultural configurations" of the family firm. A company's cultural configuration is the basis for understanding the complexities of the firm over its life cycle and will be referred to extensively in the succeeding chapters.

The various cultural patterns can be used to illustrate some of the more common cultural configurations in family businesses. For example, one cultural configuration often found in Stages 1 and 2 of the typical life cycle is a paternalistic business culture, a patriarchal family culture, and a rubber-stamp board of directors. In Stage 3, second-generation family firms, we have often found this configuration: a participative business culture, a collaborative family culture, and an advisory board; this configuration is rarely found in a first-generation family business. We also tend to see professional cultures, conflicted families, and overseer boards in Stage 4 family firms. Of course not all family firm cultures have the same evolutionary patterns, but there are common cultural patterns and problems stemming from those patterns that afflict a family business at various stages of development.

Three

Leaders as Catalysts
for Cultural Change

The histories of family firms demonstrate how vulnerable a business is to forces in the environment. In response to these pressures, the firm and family are often in flux, attempting to cope with new conditions and situations. We often find that in fact leaders of the firm, either consciously or unconsciously, sow the seeds of eventual change themselves—sometimes the seeds of destruction. Because many leaders of family firms are not aware of the consequences of their actions, most fail to plan for and manage change effectively. This lack of planning often results in sudden, revolutionary transformations that are not managed well.

In this chapter we will describe the conditions that stimulate these sudden, unplanned transformations in the business cultures of family firms, and discuss their implications for leaders of family firms. The model of culture change described in this chapter was derived from histories of family firms that had experienced significant changes in their cultures.

The Cycle of Cultural Evolution

The cycle of cultural evolution is presented in Figure 2. The model depicts the change process as composed of sequentially ordered "stages" that outline the conditions under which

Note: This chapter is adapted from "The Cycle of Cultural Evolution in Organizations," in R. Kilmann, M. Saxton, R. Serpa, and Associates, *Gaining Control of the Corporate Culture.* San Francisco: Jossey-Bass, 1985.

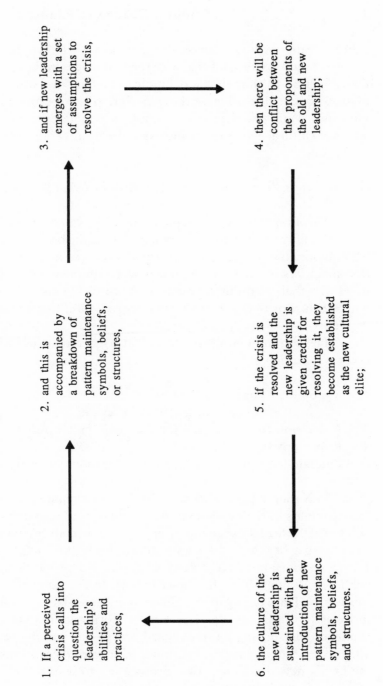

Figure 2. The Cycle of Cultural Evolution.

1. If a perceived crisis calls into question the leadership's abilities and practices,

2. and this is accompanied by a breakdown of pattern maintenance symbols, beliefs, or structures,

3. and if new leadership emerges with a set of assumptions to resolve the crisis,

4. then there will be conflict between the proponents of the old and new leadership;

5. if the crisis is resolved and the new leadership is given credit for resolving it, they become established as the new cultural elite;

6. the culture of the new leadership is sustained with the introduction of new pattern maintenance symbols, beliefs, and structures.

culture change will take place. (These "stages" in the change process should not be confused with the four stages in the family firm life cycle.) While the model indicates a temporal ordering of the stages, it is possible for them to overlap or to occur simultaneously. With this sequence in mind, we will describe the six stages of cultural evolution, using examples from various family businesses.

Stage 1: The Leadership's Abilities and Practices Are Called into Question

The first stage of the process involves questioning the leaders' ability to solve major problems facing the organization. This questioning is triggered when certain events create a "crisis" that members of the organization perceive the leaders cannot solve with their traditional practices. A search begins for alternative behavior that will enable the organization to cope with the crisis.

The common kinds of events that triggered crises in the cases we studied are:

1. Major recessions or a depression
2. Death or retirement of the founder/leader
3. A decision to merge, sell the business, or go public
4. Rapid growth
5. Fundamental changes in strategy, technology, or structure

In National Cash Register (NCR), for example, declining dividends in the 1930s caused stockholders to question the abilities of the firm's leadership, which then led to culture change. Levi Strauss began to change its culture when the company's European division lost $12 million in 1973—a period of time president Walter Haas, Jr., described as "very traumatic"— causing the Haas family to reevaluate their laissez-faire management style (Cray, 1978). The Brown Corporation's culture changed twice during its sixty-year history—once in the early 1960s after the founder retired and a poor sales record caused the firm's new president, John Brown, Jr., to search for new ideas to run the business, and again in 1973 after the worldwide recession caused sales to drop dramatically. In each of these cases a significant crisis provided the impetus to begin the process of culture change.

Stage 2: Breakdown of Pattern Maintenance Symbols, Beliefs, and Structures

When the leadership's ability to manage effectively is questioned, there may be a breakdown or loss of what we have called pattern maintenance symbols, beliefs, or structures that sustain the prevailing culture. For basic assumptions to be transformed, these must change first.

Pattern Maintenance Symbols. The term *pattern maintenance symbols* refers to those artifacts that sustain and support the prevailing culture. Such symbols serve to remind members of the organization of the importance of conforming to established practices. This may include rewarding employees who conform to the culture or the mere physical presence of the founder or other "cultural elite" in the workplace.

For example, John Patterson, the eccentric and egocentric founder of NCR, was apparently a master at enforcing his policies. Stanley Allyn, future president of the company, describes one encounter with Patterson (1967, p. 40):

> Even as excited and dedicated employee as I was had to be wary. Patterson had been known to discharge an employee merely through dislike of the way the man combed his hair. . . . One Saturday noon, certain that . . . Mr. Patterson had departed, I lit a cigar. I had taken one luxurious puff when I heard his unmistakable nervously rapid footfall in the corridor. In his later years Mr. Patterson was a rampaging tyrant about tobacco, convinced that no one was efficient with nicotine contaminating the blood. Across my room, a window was open eight or nine inches. With deadly accuracy, my job depending on my skill, I pitched out the cigar. "Who's been smoking here?" Patterson asked, his head suddenly in the door, his nose sniffing

the air like that of a basset hound. "Uh, it must have been one of the salesmen," I muttered. "No wonder business is off," Patterson growled. "Everyone is full of poison." If he had known the name of the offender, my career at NCR probably would have ended that instant.

In each case, the leader's declining ability to reinforce the company's values and assumptions with both word and deed was a key factor in culture change. John Patterson's declining health paved the way for new leadership to establish a new set of symbols that represented a different set of assumptions. In other cases the founder failed to inculcate his beliefs upon family and nonfamily employees. Because the next generation couldn't understand or articulate the founder's values, new beliefs began to emerge. In a few cases the founders became so involved in interests outside the firm—political, social, or other financial activities—that they failed to reinforce their beliefs to families and employees on a consistent basis.

Pattern Maintenance Beliefs. To sustain a given culture, leaders promulgate certain beliefs that tend to stifle any opposition that might lead to questioning the basic premises on which the culture is founded. Contradictions in a belief system or discrepancies between espoused beliefs and actual behavior are common and must somehow be mediated if the leadership is to avoid the questioning of those beliefs. Members of these organizations are taught to accept the essential "goodness" of the leader or owning family, and to believe that the leader, who has helped build and sustain the firm, will be able to cope with any emergency.

The following story told by Stanley Allyn suggests that NCR values were so deeply ingrained in employees and deemed to be so "right" that they transcended national boundaries even during times of war: "The NCR Paris office on the Champs Elysées was on the line of march when Hitler's Wehrmächt rumbled into the capital of the French in 1940. A tank swerved from the column and halted before the NCR door. Out leaped a German soldier. He pounded for admittance. Finally our French employees decided that discretion required that they open to him. The German smiled and said, "I'm from NCR in Berlin. I just wondered if you made your quota last year?" [Allyn, 1967, p. 126].

When overwhelming crises confront family firms, beliefs like "The founder is always right" or "The family will take care of its employees" can become untenable. With such core beliefs shaken, a major stumbling block to culture change is eliminated. In some cases family members or employees may begin to reject the "old philosophy" when they discover new, perhaps more useful beliefs and practices to help them cope with their problems. New employees, consultants, and other firms in the industry are often sources of new ideas, new beliefs, that can be used to supplant the firm's time-honored values.

Pattern Maintenance Structures. Certain organizational structures, such as reward systems and job design, may also sustain the culture of the organization, since they often reflect the assumptions of the culture and are difficult to change quickly. One of the most significant structural barriers to culture change in the cases we studied appears to be company ownership. Those leaders who both own and operate a business are less susceptible to outside demands for change than are those who must satisfy a number of constituencies. In some cases, such as NCR, culture change was initiated simultaneously with a change in ownership. In other cases, such as Levi Strauss and the Brown Corporation, cultures began to change within five years after the companies became publicly held. Since ownership constitutes power, any change in ownership that dilutes the power of the firm's leaders may stimulate culture change.

Stage 3: New Leadership Emerges with an Alternative Set of Assumptions

Although doubts about the leader's ability to govern and a breakdown of power-sustaining symbols, beliefs, and structures are necessary conditions for culture change to take place, they are not sufficient to trigger change. Without some alternative set of artifacts, perspectives, values, and assumptions available to test and evaluate, the organization will, in all likelihood, continue to respond to the crisis in ways that proved successful in the past.

In each company we studied, major leadership transitions provided the impetus for change. Founders often have different management styles from professional managers or others who succeed them, and these differences create different cultural patterns. For example, NCR's culture changed dramatically as Colonel Edward Deeds began to emphasize teamwork and joint decision making, in stark contrast with the autocratic and dictatorial style of John Patterson. The laissez-faire management philosophy practiced by Levi Strauss and his successors was replaced by strict controls and accountability when Robert Grohman, a company "outsider" from Playtex and B.V.D. Co., was brought in to resolve the crisis the company was facing in 1973. The Brown Corporation's culture changed twice: first the son of the founder attempted in the early 1960s to promote participative management in contrast with the autocratic paternalism that characterized his father's tenure. Then in 1974, Reed Larson replaced the participative culture with one founded on assumptions that nurtured individual initiative and a reliance on "professional" decision models.

Stage 4: Conflict—Struggle for Control
Between Proponents of Old and New Leadership

After the introduction of new leadership, a period of conflict ensues between proponents of old and new. These conflicts may be rather short-lived, or they may last for a number of years, as was the case in the Brown Corporation. The losers in such conflicts feel great resentment toward the new leaders and their values, and therefore they generally are not reeducated to the new beliefs. Most are quickly purged or leave voluntarily.

Michael Silva at Bennett Enterprises quickly fired those who opposed his new regime and replaced them with managers who fit his philosophy. Similarly, with the advent of Robert Grohman at Levi Strauss during the 1973 recession, nine of the eleven general managers in Europe and between fifty and seventy-

five lower-level managers were fired—this in a firm long known
for paternalism and an emphasis on lifetime employment. Company old-timers called Grohman's entry into Levi Strauss a
"heart transplant." He began to develop new goals and values
that emphasized strict accountability and more "impersonal"
interactions between management and employees. His primary
watchword was "don't act on your own"—quite a change from
the company's previous value on independent action. This new
set of artifacts, perspectives, values, and assumptions rapidly
transformed the Levi Strauss culture. As one old-timer complained: "Most people working here need a family type atmosphere. You need to feel involved. But now I feel like Standard
Oil or General Motors. I don't feel like I really belong to the
whole. 'You're on you own, baby. Sink or swim'" (Cray, 1978,
p. 239). As a result of these changes at Levi Strauss, "Some
of the more entrepreneurial-minded resisted Grohman's con-
stricting pressure. The one-time Levi's salesman who opened
Levi Strauss Canada and built it into a $50-million-a-year enter-
prise could not bend his traditional attitudes, declined a job offer
in the home office, and left the company. Two ranking executives
shunted aside in the reorganization of the International Group
left Levi's for other companies" (p. 226).

In the other cases, there are similar reports of nonfamily
employees, board members, and family members being fired,
voluntarily leaving, or attempting to sabotage the programs of
the new leaders. Indeed, conflict appears to be an integral part
of the process of culture change.

*Stage 5: The New Leadership Solves the Crisis
and Becomes the New Cultural Elite*

Given that the advent of new leadership and the introduction of new ideas and beliefs often create conflicts and resentment among members of an organization, the question arises:
How is the new leadership able to win the conflict and establish
a new cultural pattern? Two conditions seem to be necessary.
First, the crisis must be resolved; that is, the conditions creating
the tension and anxiety in the organization must somehow be

ameliorated. Second, the new leadership must be perceived as having resolved the crisis and must be given credit for the improvement. This success is generally linked to improved sales and profits. At Levi Strauss, the success of Grohman's new values was found in the company's annual report: "The 1974 annual report validated Grohman's efforts. They had adverted further international disasters, confining the decline to a one-quarter lapse. Despite the worldwide recession caused by the Arab oil boycott, Levi Strauss sales increased more than one-third, to $987.6 million. It was the largest increase, both in dollars and as a percentage, in corporate history" (Cray, 1978, p. 227).

Once the crisis is resolved, new leaders are often referred to as "the guys who turned things around" or the "saviors" of the firm. Because they are given credit for saving the organization from disaster, the new leaders are given tremendous power and discretion to initiate changes in the company culture.

Stage 6: New Symbols, Beliefs, and Structures
Institutionalize the New Culture

As the new leadership establishes its authority, it begins to create new symbols, beliefs, and structures to sustain the organization's culture. To symbolize their dominance, the new leaders often promote and hire only those employees who are amenable to the new culture. Nonconformists are demoted or fired. They attempt to instill in their subordinates the essential "rightness" of their beliefs. This is often done by pointing out their successes and discrediting the previous regime. History is often reinterpreted by new leaders.

John Patterson at NCR was seen by the new leadership as a "tyrannical dictator," a good leader for his time but not for a modern corporation. Robert Grohman was brought in to replace the laissez-faire management that had "failed" at Levi Strauss. And Reed Larson debunked the Brown Corporation's participative management of the 1960s, declaring it "too groupy—not tough enough." In each case, replacing old, discredited beliefs with new ideals appears to be one reliable indicator that the culture has indeed changed. (George Orwell's statement that "who controls the past controls the future [and] who controls the present controls the past" [1949, p. 32] seems quite apropos.)

New structures are often set up to sustain the new culture. In cases where professional managers are brought in to resolve the crisis, a divisional organization structure is often created. This allows the professional managers to concentrate power in a corporate headquarters and presents them with opportunities to disseminate their values by creating new divisions led by managers who support them. Ownership is also frequently restructured to bolster the position of new leadership. New leaders are given shares of company stock or stock options to increase their influence on company affairs.

In summary, this model of cultural change suggests that change is triggered by certain crises that call into question the leader's ability to govern. At the same time there is generally a breakdown of pattern maintenance symbols, beliefs, and structures that served to sustain the underlying assumptions of the "old" culture. With the advent of new leadership, a period of conflict ensues between proponents of the old and new cultures. If the crisis is resolved after the introduction of new leaders, and if members of the family and the organization attribute this success to their efforts, then this firmly establishes the new cultural pattern. The new leadership is then able to take steps to institutionalize the new culture by creating new pattern maintenance symbols, beliefs, and structures and by expelling or "converting" those who adhere to the old beliefs. The new culture is then sustained until some event again calls into question the leadership's abilities and practices, and the cycle of cultural evolution is repeated.

Implications for Managing Culture Change

This six-stage model of cultural change appears to have significant implications for current theory and practice about culture change.

Planning for Culture Change. The events that precipitate changes in the cultures of these companies typically are *not* planned for by the owning family. Unanticipated recessions, financial crises, and the illness or death of key leaders are often instrumental in triggering culture change. Serendipity and historical accidents play a critical role. While in theory it may be possible to anticipate such "accidents," managers in family firms generally fail to plan for such contingencies. The lack of succession planning or other types of contingency planning often sets up the firm and the family for great trauma and conflict.

The Role of Leadership in Culture Change. Despite the fact that certain events stimulating culture change are often uncontrollable, there are some strategic choices available to those attempting to change a culture's basic assumptions. The most important choice concerns the selection of new leaders. Leaders are often the creators and transmitters of culture. In each case cited here, the firm's board of directors had the opportunity to select the kind of leader they believed would be able to resolve the crisis.

As an alternative to replacing the leadership, it is possible to have the old leadership adopt new beliefs and values that are more compatible with the changing conditions. Nystrom and Starbuck (1984) have argued that, to avoid crises, leaders must "unlearn" previous behaviors and their underlying beliefs. While such changes are clearly possible, the experience of the firms we studied suggests that it is not likely. When faced with a crisis, the leaders generally continue to operate as they have in the past—often with more vigor than before. When leaders wear such blinders, the problem often intensifies.

We found that one of the common features of the firms that experienced major transformations in their cultures was the success of each new leader who emerged during a crisis. After the new leader's arrival, each company's sales and profits rose within a few months or years. Because economic conditions precipitated many of the crises and because the economy improved after each introduction of new leaders, we cannot tell whether the actions of the new leaders were directly or indirectly responsible for the improvement. What is clear, however, is that the leaders *believed* they were responsible for the company's success, and they *convinced company employees* that they should be given credit for the improvements. Correct or not, this belief enhanced the power of the new leaders. Thus new leaders entering an organization that has encountered a crisis are in a particularly powerful position to initiate change—members of the organization are looking for new ideas to resolve the crisis and the new leader is likely to receive credit for any successes, even though outside factors may be more significant than his actions. The combination of a crisis and new leadership provides fertile ground for initiating culture change in a family firm.

Crisis and Leadership Paradoxes. As the cycle of cultural evolution suggests, culture change is precipitated by a crisis. However, many times the family firms in our panel faced a crisis but the culture did *not* change. In fact, when the organization overcame the crisis, the prevailing artifacts, perspectives, values, and assumptions were not undermined *but further solidified.* Resolving the crisis reaffirmed their validity and usefulness, hence the culture was reinforced. In Levi Strauss, there are many heroic tales of how Levi and his descendants were able to overcome potentially devastating crises, such as the San Francisco earthquake of 1906, and save the firm from disaster. Similar stories are told in other family firms as well. The family's ability to weather such crises serves to strengthen the bonds of loyalty and commitment to the family and the culture that has been created. Thus, paradoxically, a crisis can either undermine or strengthen cultural values.

There were also a number of times throughout the histories of these firms when the leadership changed but the culture did not. Succession by itself did not produce change. In times when the organization prospered, new leaders were generally selected on the basis of whether they espoused the established beliefs that had led to prosperity. Conformity to honored beliefs, not new ideas, was valued. Thus leadership succession, rather than a harbinger of change, can be a celebration of shared beliefs; the new leader is a symbol of continuity, not change.

Thus by itself neither a crisis nor leadership succession is a clear indicator that culture change is taking place. *Both must occur in concert;* one without the other is not sufficient to trigger change.

Conflict and Culture Change. As the model of culture change illustrates, the change process is fraught with conflict—managers are fired, employees quit, struggles for power within the family are common. Fundamental changes in organizational cultures always accompany changes in the way power is distributed. Some members of the business and the family gain by culture change, others lose. Hence the potential losers fight vigorously to maintain the status quo, to sustain the values and beliefs on which their positions are based. Because they are unwilling to part with their own beliefs and submit to the ideology of the new leaders—to relinquish their power—purges of the ''old guard'' are more common than socialization to a new set of beliefs.

One key element of culture change connected to the problem of power redistribution and conflict concerns eliminating key symbols, beliefs, or structures sustaining the culture. This may be done systematically if the new leader can identify the symbols, beliefs, and stuctures that reinforce the prevailing culture, and can determine to what extent these factors can be modified or eliminated. The conflicts inherent in such an undertaking will undoubtedly be great.

Culture Change and Adaptation. The companies that have been highlighted illustrate a variety of different cultures. Some are founded on assumptions fostering founder domination and control. Others create more egalitarian relationships and reflect a high degree of trust between members of the organization. Although we are dealing with a relatively small number of cases, an examination of the relationship between culture and organizational effectiveness reveals that no one pattern is associated with a successful organization in the short run. John Patterson was successful at NCR with a highly autocratic culture, while his successor, Edward Deeds, was successful by developing an amiable team. With a laissez-faire orientation, Levi Strauss & Co. grew quickly. The Brown Corporation grew steadily under both autocratic and participative management, while Bennett Enterprises' financial condition was stabilized under the direction of Michael Silva.

Nor should we assume that all cultural patterns have similar consequences in the long run. For example, the three cultural patterns witnessed in the Brown Corporation had varying effects. The culture during the tenure of founder John Brown, Sr., which emphasized founder and family dominance, fostered a high degree of dependency among Brown's employees. With most of the power and knowledge about the firm's operations in the hands of John, Sr., his subordinates had few opportunities to exercise independent action or magnify their managerial abilities. This pattern can leave the firm in a rather precarious position. The sudden departure of the founder could prove chaotic; indeed, the illness of John, Sr., in the late 1940s posed a serious problem for the firm and the family. The culture of that period allowed for little development of subordinates, and the dependence on the founder for direction made the firm vulnerable if the founder were to die or be disabled. However, the leadership abilities of John, Sr., and a favorable economic climate were largely responsible for the company's success during the 1940s and 1950s.

The culture at Brown during the 1960s, on the other hand, fostered both independence and collaboration. This proved to be useful when the company's growth in the 1960s made coordinating the various subunits a key problem. By delegating authority, lower-level managers expanded their ability to act independently, and this mixture of high collaboration and freedom seems to be related to a number of managerial and technical innovations developed during this period.

The culture nurtured by the professional manager Reed Larson had a different set of consequences. With "efficiency" as the salient criterion, Larson attempted to improve the organization's performance. Controls were installed and "dead wood" eliminated. The focus was more on individual achievement and less on participation. These measures appear to have helped the company weather the recession in the early 1970s. Under this cultural pattern, efficiency (based on the company's measures) seems to have improved. However, worker turnover and dissatisfaction also increased, and the company has not been as innovative.

In summary, although each cultural pattern does have different consequences for the organization and the people in it, no single pattern appears necessarily related to organizational growth, market share, sales, profits, or other such criteria of organizational effectiveness. Environmental and internal conditions dictate the kind of culture appropriate for a given situation (Hershon, 1975). The Brown Corporation, for instance, adapted its cultural pattern to respond to changes in business strategy and to changes within the family. However, most family firms do not adapt their cultures to meet changing times. Firms with cultural patterns that inhibit planning and hamper successful transitions are likely to experience a serious crisis at some point in their history.

ᏒᏣᏲᎬᎭᏦᏣᏲᎬᎭᏦᏣᏲᎬᎭᏦᏣᏲᎬᎭᏦᏣᏲᎬᎭᏦᏣᏲᎬᎭᏦᏣᏲᎬᎭᏗ

Anticipating Cultural Transitions from Generation to Generation

In Part One the family firm life cycle, family firm cultural patterns, and process of culture change were discussed. In Part Two, we will turn our attention to specific cultural problems that are found at the various stages of a family firm's development. Because these problems are frequently created by the cultural configuration of a family firm, they have been defined as being "cultural" in nature.

In Chapter Four, the problems associated with cultures found during the founder's tenure are presented. Since founders are often the "creators" of culture and shape the values of the institutions they build, it is important to understand the personality traits that lead them to create particular kinds of cultures. Founders often create cultures that emphasize their own power and influence. They are unwilling to delegate responsibility and tend to keep subordinates highly dependent upon them for direction. Such cultural patterns make it difficult for the firm to survive beyond the first generation. Chapter Four describes these problems and provides some suggestions for managing them.

Chapter Five describes the conflicts and power struggles generally found in second- and third-generation family firms. Because of the diversity of interests among family members in succeeding generations, the family must be able to create a "collective vision" to ensure continuity. This chapter also discusses some of the pitfalls for leaders in the second and third generation and suggests some mechanisms that can be used to minimize conflict after the founder departs.

Only a few family firms get to the point in their development where they must bring in "professional" management;

fewer still offer their stock to the public. However, for these few, these two transitions are crucial, and Chapter Six discusses their impact. Leaders of family firms generally have a number of "good" reasons to go public or bring in professional management, but they are generally not aware of many of the unintended consequences of these actions. The cultures of family firms change dramatically—often with negative results for the family. Several case studies illustrate what can happen when the family firm moves to this final stage in its life cycle.

Four

The First Generation:
How the Founder
Shapes the Culture

The problems that founders and their families face is graphically illustrated by the case of William Millard at ComputerLand. Millard built a billion-dollar empire with 1,100 employees and 800 franchisees in a few short years. As the majority stockholder, he ruled with an iron hand; he promoted his daughter Barbara to president in 1984 over a number of more seasoned managers. Both Millards are now out of the business—forced to resign by disgruntled investors and angry franchisees.

The crux of the problem seemed to be William Millard's inability to listen to and work with others and make needed changes in the firm's strategy. Investors claimed that Millard reneged on an agreement to deliver stock to them; franchisees believed that the Millards were not treating them fairly. New competitors such as Entré Computer Centers began to capture market share from ComputerLand. One of ComputerLand's franchisees complained, "It's because of Bill's arrogance that all the problems came about" ("All in the Family," p. 68).

Like William Millard, most founders have blinders on. They are unwilling to listen to advice, collaborate with others, or recognize their own weaknesses. Thus they unknowingly get themselves, their families, and their businesses in deep trouble by fostering cultural patterns that are not amenable to change.

In this chapter we will

1. Examine the personal characteristics of founders that tend to reinforce certain kinds of cultures.

59

2. Describe the kind of cultural configurations frequently created by such leaders.
3. Identify some of the problems associated with these configurations.
4. Discuss some of the ways of avoiding these problems.

Founders: The Creators of Culture

One of the most significant factors in the development of the cultural configurations of the family firms we studied was the presence of a strong, charismatic founder. In the early part of the twentieth century, Max Weber first wrote about these leaders, indicating that they had extraordinary powers to create a "vision" for their followers and to instill in them a religious fervor in carrying out their dream. The founders of family firms play the dominant role in shaping the institutions that they create. One cannot study family businesses without noticing the effects of the leadership of men like Thomas Watson, John Patterson, Willard Marriott, and Levi Strauss.

Founder Characteristics. Founders of family firms share many goals, values, and ideals. Many writers have attempted to describe the attributes that founders often share; for example, see McClelland (1961), Zaleznick (1977), Kets de Vries (1977), Schein (1983), and Kets de Vries and Miller (1984). In a recent review of the literature on leadership and charisma, Trice and Beyer (1985) summarized much of the work in this area. They noted that charismatic founders are generally seen *as claiming* supernatural or other transcendental qualities that are almost magical in nature. Followers are drawn by this magnetism because the leaders have a novel or even radical program that satisfies the followers' basic needs and desires. These leaders often emerge during times of crisis because they are able to solve the crisis, thus becoming the "saviors" for their followers. Individual character traits, the motives of the followers, and the nature of the situation all combine to produce this kind of leadership.

House (1977) further delineates some of the key attributes of these charismatic leaders: "extremely high levels of self confidence, dominance, and a strong conviction in the moral righteousness of his/her beliefs'' (p. 194). They are also able to (1) effectively role model; (2) create impressions of competence and success; (3) articulate ideological goals; (4) communicate high expectations plus confidence in followers; and (5) generate motive-arousing behaviors (pp. 194–203). Thus in both word and deed we often find founders communicating the "rightness" of their visions and motivating their followers to action, for acting in accordance with the leader's wishes can bring salvation, either temporally or spiritually.

In addition, founders of family businesses, in general, tend to

1. Distrust other authority figures.
2. Be self-reliant.
3. Reject advice from others.
4. Exercise power in seemingly arbitrary and capricious ways.
5. Be secretive about their activities.
6. Totally organize and control both business and family activities.
7. Be reluctant to delegate to others.
8. Develop a philosophy that is followed implicitly.
9. Be portrayed by themselves and others as "larger than life."

Given this set of attributes, family firm cultures in the first generation are quite different (as we shall see) from those developed in succeeding generations.

To illustrate how such founders shape the values of their organizations, let us look at one highly successful example— John H. Patterson, founder of National Cash Register, "the father of modern salesmanship."

John H. Patterson: Portrait of a Founder. John Henry Patterson was born December 13, 1844, on a farm in Ohio. John learned, at an early age, the value of hard work, frequently working from 4:00 A.M. until well into the evening. The son of a rather prominent family, John was given the opportunity to attend Miami University at Oxford. His time there was brief, however, because his father died shortly after he enrolled and he had to return home to run the farm in 1863. His three brothers were in the Army, and one brother, William, died as a result of injuries received in the Civil War. After the war ended, John enrolled in college again, this time at Dartmouth, and graduated with a bachelor of arts degree in 1867. Of his Dartmouth experience, Patterson once remarked: "What I learned mostly was what not to do. They gave me Greek and Latin and algebra and higher mathematics and Edwards on the Will—all useless" (Crowther, 1923, p. 29). Throughout his life Patterson was wary of those who held college degrees.

Back home from Dartmouth, Patterson discovered that there was little demand for someone with a college degree, and he ended up with the rather menial task of collecting tolls at the local canal. Such a job was unbearable for someone with Patterson's ambition, and it drove him into what has been described as a "desperation for accomplishment" (Crowther, 1923, p. 3). In response to this monotonous work, Patterson started a wood and coal business on the side in a partnership with his brothers, Stephen and Frank. Six years later he quit as a toll collector and began managing the business full time. After eight years the three brothers controlled one-half of Dayton's retail coal business and had an interest in a number of coal mines. But he wanted more adventure.

In 1884 Patterson paid $6,500 for the controlling interest in the National Manufacturing Company, a company that had acquired the patent for the cash register. Patterson quickly changed the name to National Cash Register, and the company began its meteoric rise.

Patterson charted his own course when he took over NCR. He ignored precedents and rarely listened to advice from local business leaders. He believed that advertising and salesmanship were the keys to success and developed the most sophisticated training school for salesmen in his day. The salesmen learned Patterson's philosophy from the NCR "primer." They wore white shirts and dark suits—a forerunner of the IBM image. In fact, Thomas Watson and a host of other successful salesmen received their initial training at NCR. Patterson's salesmen were known for ruthlessness. For example: "[One NCR] salesman cracked one of the Midwest's largest department stores with nothing but brashness. The management insisted that cash registers were unnecessary, because a system of merchandise inspection prevented dishonesty or mistakes. The salesman moved stealthily around the dry good department one day, and switched all the price tags, putting $20 tags on $40 suits and vice versa. No one noticed his occupation. Then he went to the owner. 'Your inspection isn't worth a damn,' he said, 'and I've proved it.' The store fired its inspectors and converted to NCR's system" (Allyn, 1967, pp. 77, 78).

Another time NCR was facing stiff competition from other companies that were selling refurbished cash registers. To combat this threat, Patterson ordered Thomas Watson and a few other managers to set up a company—to be funded by NCR—that would sell the secondhand cash registers at cost. This move effectively destroyed the competition, but it was obviously illegal. The competition filed suit, and Patterson and twenty-seven of his top managers—including Thomas Watson—were found guilty. Patterson appealed. In the interim, a terrible flood engulfed Dayton. Patterson mustered all the company's resources to feed the hungry and homeless. In the wake of the public support that followed, Patterson won his appeal and was given a large victory parade in Dayton. However, the more than two dozen managers who also won their appeals—including Thomas Watson—were summarily fired.

Patterson developed an elaborate philosophy that was embodied in eighty-five statements prominently displayed at the company, and he created an entire department whose sole purpose was to spread this philosophy throughout the company. To further emphasize his beliefs, he would carefully stage events, like smashing a defective cash register to make a point. He left nothing to chance: "He staged every demonstration. . . . If he wanted to be interrupted by questions before a convention or a factory meeting, he arranged for the interruptions in advance. For instance, in a meeting where he was trying to drive home the importance of speaking in simple, exact language, he hesitated to find a word and in his apparent confusion he snapped: 'Will somebody give me the word I want?' Somebody did, and he tossed him a twenty-dollar gold piece. It was not necessary further to demonstrate the value of language to that meeting" (Crowther, 1923, pp. 14, 15).

He also engaged in a number of rather unusual behaviors that would keep his subordinates off balance. He would give an employee a raise one week and fire him the next. One company story tells of a manager coming to work only to find his desk burning in a nearby field—a clear sign that he was in trouble. Another more subtle sign was that Patterson would mispronounce your name. If he *forgot* your name, you could start looking for another job.

Patterson viewed himself as a pioneer or a conqueror. He rode a white horse because Napoleon did. He claimed to be an expert in topics ranging from health to religion and took every opportunity to expound upon and demonstrate his beliefs. He created one of the first "welfare" industrial organizations in the United States. An NCR employee's entire life was centered around the company, and Patterson built a variety of amenities such as parks and theaters to bring the employee's family into the NCR fold. He was a classic paternalist in the best sense of the word: "He was intent on helping, not on pauperizing, and he was so intent on helping that often he insisted on minutely regulating the lives of those with whom he came in contact. He was perfectly willing to override the objections of the individuals if he believed that the individual's objections were . . . against the best interests both of the individual and of society. He thought there was only one best way of doing anything and that everyone ought to be taught that best way and then be forced to follow it" (Crowther, 1923, p. 9).

This paternalistic attitude instilled a fierce loyalty to Patterson and the company. Despite his faults, no one could question his success. Armed with little money but with a wealth of drive and ambition, he had created one of the great corporations in the United States by the time he died in 1922. Like many founders, Patterson was an enigma. His followers did not always understand him, but they viewed him with awe and reverence. As one observer concluded: "He was human in his

frailties and again he was unhuman. At every point he was like
the average man and yet unlike him. He was a continual con-
tradiction of himself'' (Crowther, 1923, p. 17).

Institutionalizing the Founder's Values

Founders such as John Patterson would be only interesting
curiosities if it were not for the profound effect they have on
the organizations they create. While founders bring with them
a set of assumptions that they impose on others, they develop
other assumptions as they solve various internal and external
problems. The solutions to these problems then become an integral part of the business culture.

Founders attain an aura of success as they develop a distinctive competence for their organization that allows it to compete
successfully in the marketplace. One of the common features of
the founders we studied was their ability to take a good idea—
often an idea not their own—and implement it with a passion.
To fulfill the organization's mission and goals, they would recruit,
socialize, and train both family and nonfamily members to carry
out key functions. The culture as created and sustained by the
founder also served to integrate members of the organization to
work cooperatively together. The founder's vision helped to create
a sense of meaning and direction for the employees' work lives,
and this vision often extended into their family lives as well.

The influence of these founders on the organizations they
create and the workers they employ is pervasive, and is strength-
ened by a number of tactics to embed and transmit their values.
Our studies and the recent work of Edgar Schein (1983, 1985)
describe some of these tactics, including:

1. Creating a written philosophy that is well known and shared
   by members of the family and the organization.
2. Using opportunities to demonstrate dramatically how the
   philosophy ''works.''
3. Recruiting, rewarding, and promoting those employees who
   behave consistently with the founder's beliefs.

4. Avoiding reviews or critiques of the founder's actions. Dissenters are severely punished or banished from the organization.
5. Using stories, legends, rituals, employee dress, or other artifacts to remind others of the nature and purpose of their "mission."
6. Creating organizational systems, procedures, and structures that reflect the core assumptions of the founder.

Founders may attempt other techniques to embed a particular cultural pattern in a business, but these seem to be the most common.

Once a founder embeds his or her values in the organization's mission, goals, and structures, and effectively transmits them to employees, the organization often takes on its own identity and becomes what Philip Selznick (1957) refers to as an "institution" that becomes "infused with value," over and above its rational value of carrying out the founder's mission. The organization was initially set up to serve certain ends, but as institutionalization sets in, preserving the organization *becomes* the end, for it is the symbol of the founder's philosophy and of the group's uniqueness. The leaders of such institutions are seen as the "protectors" and "promoters" of the core assumptions and values. Given this natural movement toward institutionalization in the early stages of the development of a family business, the culture created by charismatic leaders can prove to be highly resistant to change.

Founder Influence on
Family and Governance Cultures

Many of the same processes of creating and sustaining the founder's values in the business—creating a philosophy, demonstrating its value, rewarding followers, and punishing antagonists—also take place in the family and governing boards. There are, however, some issues unique to the family and the governing boards that require the founder's attention. How the founder and family resolve these issues and the assumptions behind them is often the key to understanding the cultural configuration of the family firm. For the family, some of the issues include:

1. Who is considered to be family? What should be the role of in-laws, stepbrothers/sisters, and so on? Who is "in" and who is "out?"
2. What should be the criteria of "success" in the family—birth order, training, experience, or competence?
3. What should our relationship be with one another—hierarchical, conflicted, or collaborative?
4. How do we solve problems and make decisions?
5. What is our relationship to the business?

There are, of course, many different answers to these questions, and different answers reflect different assumptions about relationships, human nature, power and authority, and the nature of truth.

The culture of the governing board, as established by the founder, is often underpinned by the answers to such questions as:

1. What should be the role and function of the board—rubberstamp, advisory, paper, or overseer?
2. Who should be on the board?
3. How should the family's assets be used?
4. What issues and problems should be handled by the board? What issues are not in the board's domain?
5. What should be the process for arriving at a decision?

Again, the answers to these questions may be many and varied, and they are crucial to the creation of the various cultural configurations that were discussed in Chapter Two.

Cultural Configurations in the First Generation

Up to now we have focused on the importance of the founder's role in creating, shaping, and institutionalizing the cultural patterns found in the firm, the family, and the governing bodies. Given the kinds of attributes connected with founders, it is not surprising that they foster similar cultural configurations.

The most common configuration we found consisted of a paternalistic organization, a patriarchal family, and a rubber-stamp board. IBM, National Cash Register, and the Brown Corporation are just a few examples of this pattern. This configuration is highly consistent. Members of the organization share the founder's vision and give him loyalty and obedience. In return, the founder nurtures, supports, and guides his followers. The founder also plays the central role in the family; all authority rests in the founder and family members are dependent upon him for direction. The board's role is to rubber stamp the founder's policies—not change them.

Another common configuration consists of a paternalistic business organization, a conflicted family, and either a rubber-stamp or advisory board. In this configuration, the founder still rules the firm with an autocratic hand but finds resistance to his power and authority within the family. Father-son conflicts and sibling rivalries are common. Major power struggles like those that occurred at Genesco between Maxey Jarman and his son Frank characterize this kind of organization.

In summary, first-generation founders generally create a paternalistic organization, and have either a conflicted or patriarchal family. The governing boards are an extension of the founder's power. We found few professional or participative firm cultures, and a collaborative family was rare in the first generation. In a few cases where venture capitalists were involved or there was significant outside ownership, the company had an overseer board.

One of the more unusual first-generation family businesses we discovered was W. L. Gore & Associates. Founded in the late 1950s by Bill Gore, a scientist from Du Pont who developed various applications for Teflon, the company has created a distinctive participative culture. The advantages of such a culture seem to include high commitment and morale among employees, the ability to respond quickly to a changing environment, and the ability to develop competent employees—the Gore family does not feel that it must constantly monitor each employee.

All 4,000 employees are called "associates." Terms like *boss, manager,* or *supervisor* are replaced with *leader* or *sponsor.* Overt perks or status symbols are disdained. There are no job descriptions, organization charts, or formal hierarchy, and the associates can become part owners of the company after one year of service. Bob Gore, Bill's son and the current president, constantly reinforces the belief that status, rules, and hierarchy inhibit communication and group decision making (Pacanowski, personal communication to author, June 28, 1985). The company is committed to an egalitarian ethic and the Gore family has attempted to instill in its workers a sense of freedom plus responsibility that is seldom found in a family-owned business, particularly one whose founder is still active. As W. L. Gore and Associates demonstrates, founders can create a participative culture during their lifetimes; however, because most founders have strong needs for power and control, this pattern is the rare exception.

The Problems of the Founder Culture

The predominant cultural configurations that we discovered in the first-generation family firm have a number of implications for the continued growth and survival of the business. There are some advantages. Employee loyalty and commitment to the founder's vision are high. Power and authority are not problematic; no one ever has to wonder where the power lies. If decisions need to be made quickly to meet certain contingencies, the founder can move swiftly to mobilize the firm's resources. Many family firms are able to survive in Stage I because the founder is knowledgeable, hard-working, and resourceful.

The disadvantages of such cultural patterns are, however, significant. Problems tend to arise as the business develops beyond Stage 1. As the business and family grow and mature, the founder's assumptions fail to "work." We will examine six fairly common and quite critical problems.

Overreliance on the Founder for Direction. We can illustrate the problem of relying too heavily on the founder for direction with an example from the ancient Incas. They had developed a highly advanced civilization that stretched almost the length of South America. Their art, architecture, and science were, in many ways, more advanced than the Europeans. But the Spanish conquistador Pizarro was able to conquer this vast empire and subjugate hundreds of thousands of its inhabitants with only 106 soldiers and 50 horses. How? Why?

The Incas believed that their rulers were descendants of the gods. They believed that all truth, knowledge, and direction flowed from their ruler and relied on him totally for direction. When Pizarro heard this, he realized that controlling the king was the key to success. Using an elaborate scheme, he kidnapped the king and forced him to order his people to do the conquistador's bidding. In a short time, Pizarro was in complete control, for the Incas were unable to organize themselves effectively to combat the new enemy. Without their leader, they were lost.

Pizarro's success demonstrates the key weakness of paternalistic cultures frequently found in first-generation family firms. Without the founder to organize and coordinate activities, the followers are lost. The dependence that founders create in their subordinates prevents them from acting independently and developing into competent managers. Furthermore, crucial contacts with clients, suppliers, and other stakeholders may be lost if the founder suddenly dies or is incapacitated. This dependent relationship leaves the family and the firm in a highly vulnerable position.

Slow Reaction to New Competitive Environments. Founders create an organization to fulfill certain needs and desires, and they set up structures and motivate employees to carry out their vision. Problems arise, however, when the environment changes and the company's goods or services are no longer valued in the marketplace. Because founders are often so committed to their mission (and that is what they know and do well), they are reluctant to experiment and often deny that anything is going wrong. Their emphasis either on present results or on past triumphs directs them away from planning for the future and meeting new contingencies. They frequently realize too late the need to change. And even if they do, they have by then created an organization designed to accomplish an obsolete set of goals. Redirecting the efforts of employees can prove overwhelming.

Inefficient Decision-Making Processes. We also find poor decision making in first-generation family firms. Because the founder may be seen as the only one who can make major decisions, decision making either gets delayed or constantly pushed up to higher levels. Employees or family members are afraid to make decisions without the founder's approval. As decisions get pushed up to the top, the data often get filtered, bad news is screened out, and the founder ends up either making a decision that should have been made at lower levels or making a decision based on biased and incomplete information. Furthermore, because founders are often reluctant to have a governing board review their decisions, there are no checks and balances. Without an outside perspective to give the decisions a "reality check" to keep the business on course, there is the strong possibility that the business will join the 70 percent of those that fail in the first generation. In a number of cases, we have seen founders who, because of poor information or because of age and senility, make decisions that destroy the business.

Lack of Adequate Training and Development. The lack of a training and development program for future leaders is a serious problem in most first-generation family firms. Many founders are consumed with the problems afflicting them in the present. Little time is taken to coach the company's future leaders. In paternalistic organizations the founders rarely delegate, so employees have few opportunities to develop their own ideas and use their discretion. Nonfamily members are generally not considered for top-management positions. They find being "second-class citizens" a frustrating experience, and many leave. It is not uncommon to find relatively unambitious, mediocre talent in the ranks of middle management in a family business.

A consultant's report to the top management of the Brown Corporation is a good example of this problem: "[John Brown, Sr.'s] attitude toward his employee has been very much that of the father toward his children. . . . The children of a forceful, effective, and loving father are quite willing to accept his exercise of broad power over their lives, with the feeling that their futures are secure in his hands. They will admire and respect him; they will have faith and trust in him. However, precisely because of his effectiveness and his positive attitudes, they will experience difficulty in escaping from his influence, in becoming independent adults'' (Dyer, 1984a, p. 71).

Unfortunately for many first-generation family businesses, the next generation is never allowed to "grow up" and become independent. When the founder dies or retires, there is an inevitable leadership crisis.

Feelings of Inadequacy and Incompetence by Family Members. Many family members experience feelings of inferiority as they watch and compare themselves to a powerful founder. The founder's children often experience the greatest pressure to succeed. Those who feel such pressures typically react in one of two ways. They may have great resentment toward the founder because they feel "victimized" by the situation. They usually leave the business and become estranged from the family because of the uncomfortable position they find themselves in. Or they may develop "self-handicapping" strategies, engaging in self-destructive behaviors—taking drugs, drinking too much, failing to achieve in school—to create "handicaps" or scapegoats for themselves. If a role model—the founder—is vastly superior and unreachable, those who try to emulate the model must have some excuse if they fail—which they are almost certain to do: they probably cannot found another successful company. By engaging in destructive behaviors, the person can point to some external factor—drugs, alcohol, poor teachers—as the cause of the problem, thus avoiding personal responsibility for his or her actions. Either approach—estrangement or self-handicapping—is a serious problem.

The Problem of Powerlessness. In the first generation, all the power tends to be concentrated in a single individual: the founder. Along with their charismatic qualities, founders have the power to reward and punish others; they have formal authority; they have certain expertise, information, and connections with key clients that make them indispensable. On the other hand, other players in the family firm system—the spouse of the founder, the children, the in-laws, nonfamily employees—have relatively few power bases from which to operate. While they may form coalitions to fight or protect themselves against the power of the founder, they find themselves in fairly weak positions.

Furthermore, founders generally do all they can to avoid sharing their power. One of the most common tactics is to cloak their activities in secrecy. Many founders are very skillful at this. By sidestepping public review of their actions, they are able to avoid criticism, maintaining the appearance that all is going well.

Maintaining an ownership position is also crucial to keeping power. In one family business that involves many families and shareholders, the head of one family has set up a trust that controls a large block of company stock. The family head is therefore able to vote the stock as a block, thus enhancing his power as well as his family's. Without such a trust, the shares might have become widely distributed and the power of the family leader diluted. Still other founders maintain their power by creating new dependencies to replace those that are no longer workable. For example, if a family member's ownership power is lessened after the firm goes public, he might try to gain some additional expertise, information, or connections to remain influential. In any case, founders of family businesses generally understand their power bases and develop strategies to either create new sources of power or enhance the ones they already have.

Because founders or other family leaders are the center of power in a family business, there are many who have little power and share a sense of powerlessness. Rosabeth Kanter (1977) has described a number of the effects of powerlessness on individuals in large bureaucracies. The symptoms of powerlessness are found in many family firms, although perhaps manifested in somewhat different ways.

Powerless individuals in family businesses suffer from feelings of self-doubt and a lower sense of self-esteem—compounding the feelings of inadequacy and incompetence described above. In terms of managerial style, we often find powerless people engaging in highly controlling behaviors. Subordinates are closely monitored and superivsed. It is as if the powerless are afraid to lose the little power they have left, so they guard it jealously.

They are also much less willing to delegate responsibility or spend time coaching and developing their subordinates. Subordinates are viewed as a threat—potential rivals—rather than a resource to be developed. The powerless may also create small islands or kingdoms from which they guard against any intruders. This makes any form of collaboration or joint decision making virtually impossible. They avoid dealing with any bad news that might endanger their position, which means that open communication is stifled and negative feedback avoided. In this "climate of powerlessness," sycophants, rather than meaningful contributors, are often rewarded, and collaboration, so essential to successful transitions, is undermined.

Managing the Problems of the Founder Culture

Avoiding the problems of the founder culture is indeed a difficult task. Most of the family firms we studied fell into a number of the pitfalls described above, and in some cases this led to the downfall of the business and the breakup of the family. There are, however, some options available for founders who wish to avoid or at least mitigate the effects of these problems.

Gain Self-Insight About the Impact of Behavior. Some of the problems can be attributed to the fact that the founders are not aware how their behavior is affecting others. To solve this may require setting up an advisory or overseer board to give the founder feedback from outsiders who can view the family business more or less objectively. Periodic "sensing" meetings, where the founder meets with family members or nonfamily employees to gain feedback about his performance, can also prove useful. In certain cases, an analysis of the founder's behavior and the firm's culture by outside consultants may be helpful (this will be discussed in greater detail in Chapter Eight). Serving as directors of *other* family firms may be another means to give founders some insights, as they have the opportunity to look at problems other families are facing. In other cases the founder may wish to attend a sensitivity training session or even engage in therapy to gain more self-awareness.

Clarify Roles and Expectations. Another possible approach is to begin to clarify roles and expectations among the founder, his or her family, and key nonfamily managers. Problems often arise when people are unclear about their responsibilities and their future roles. To reduce this uncertainty and confusion, founders might meet with key family and nonfamily members, discuss their roles, and explore the roles and expectations that they have for others (this approach will be explored in greater depth in Chapter Five).

Create a "Buffer" Between the Founder and the Organization. In some cases the founder may be unwilling or unable to gain self-insight or clarify roles in the firm. A third option is to create a "buffer" level of management which will follow the founder's overall philosophy but also create some new behavior patterns more consistent with the family's and the business' needs. For example, in the case of the Western Freight Company described in Chapter Two, the founder, Pearson, is creating all kinds of problems by meddling in the affairs of his employees. And he is unlikely to change his style. To manage this problem, Pearson might appoint a "superintendent" to supervise employees on a daily basis. Pearson could remove himself from day-to-day affairs and concentrate on broader strategic problems and key external relationships. Finding a competent manager to provide a buffer by correctly interpreting the founder's wishes and yet carrying them out in ways that are more acceptable to members of the family and the organization is another possible approach to some founder-related problems.

Create Interdependent Relationships. Creating interdependent rather than counterdependent or dependent relationships is another option. The core feature of an interdependent relationship is its reciprocal nature. The founders and others are able to influence one another *mutually*. This means that power must be shared and delegated, something family leaders usually find difficult. However, if power continues to be concentrated in only one or two individuals, as is often the case, the likelihood that the successor will be well prepared to manage the business is greatly diminished. The question is not *whether* to share power, but when and how.

Those in family firms who have been successful in exercising power have cultivated a variety of power bases. Thus it is important for the family to encourage family members who want to join the business as well as nonfamily employees to generate legitimate power bases from which to influence others.

The question often facing members of the family firm is: How do I become more influential? For those in such a situation, there are some successful strategies. Individuals lower in the firm's hierarchy often must rely on technical or managerial expertise to gain influence. Training each new generation of the Haas family at Harvard Business School helped the children gain needed skills and gave them credibility in Levi Strauss and in the business community. Others have been successful in gaining power by positioning themselves in the organizational hierarchy where they have access to important information. In some firms, family members choose to become lawyers or accountants because they realize that people in those positions often find themselves privy to information that increases the importance of their roles.

In the absence of information or expertise, forming coalitions or creating connections with key individuals both inside and outside the company may be the only other potential power base. Michael Silva at Bennett Enterprises has been able to create a strong power base for himself by forming key relationships both inside and outside the organization. He has formed a strong relationship with Wallace Bennett, the most powerful figure in the organization, and has demonstrated to the leaders of the financial institutions supporting Bennett's that he is indispensable to company operations. With their support, he, as a nonfamily manager in what had been a family-dominated enterprise, has been able to do many things to change the organization that no one thought possible.

Delegating authority and responsibility can also serve to empower others and create interdependent relationships. The most common problem in this regard is not delegating enough authority to carry out the responsibility. In some of the cases we studied, family and nonfamily members were given what appeared to be important titles by the founder, but in reality they held little power. For example, John Brown, Sr., founder of the Brown Corporation, designed a formal organization chart to give more authority to his son. As Figure 3 implies, all key

Figure 3. Official Structure of the Brown Corporation in Early 1950s.

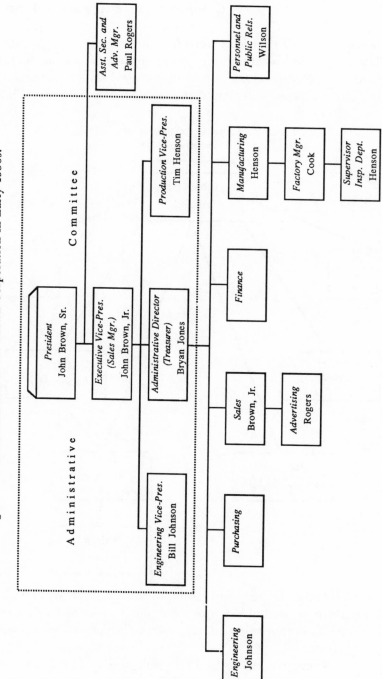

information and decisions were designed to go through John Brown, Jr., to his father. However, an analysis of the actual patterns of interaction (see Figure 4) reveals that all communication and influence still flowed through John Brown, Sr. This

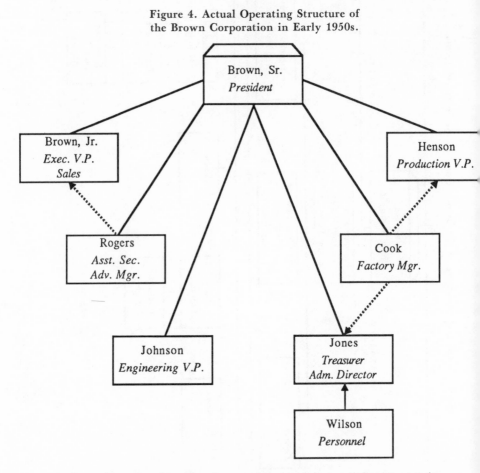

Figure 4. Actual Operating Structure of the Brown Corporation in Early 1950s.

often proved to be very frustrating to the son, who was trying to abide by the formal structure. A founder cannot merely give someone an empty title and expect other people to behave accordingly.

Not only should authority be delegated, but the tasks to be accomplished should be clearly defined. The person delegating the tasks should also provide the necessary resources and coaching to support the person and develop a timetable to follow up and receive an accounting of the stewardship that has been delegated. While these principles seem quite simple, it is remarkable how many managers of family businesses fail to follow them. Failure to delegate properly hinders the work of the organization and leaves people frustrated and unprepared to assume leadership roles.

One final issue for founders who want to create interdependent relationships concerns the power bases used during the firm's life cycle. In the early stages of a firm, we often find founders using their power bases of ownership, formal authority, charisma, or reward/punishment power. While such power bases are often very effective and many times necessary, given the importance of the founder's role in the success of the business, they put those influenced in a highly dependent position. They have few resources to "fight back" or to influence the founder. Interdependent relationships, however, must be created as the family and business mature in order to manage continuity effectively. To achieve such a relationship the founder must rely on different power bases: expertise, experience, clear information, logic, and mutual respect. Founders or other family leaders must be willing to change the kinds of power bases they use at different stages in the firm's evolution if they are adequately to prepare the next generation for leadership.

Five

Conflicts and Power Struggles in the Second and Third Generations

The cultural configurations of a family business during the founder's reign are relatively stable because of the founder's ability to create an institution that is highly resistant to change. Both family members and nonfamily employees generally are strongly committed to the founder and his ideals. As undisputed leaders of both the family and the firm, founders wield tremendous power and are thus able to quell disturbances in the business and the family and are also able to vanquish any rivals. But this may not always be so in succeeding generations. In this chapter we will explore the dynamics of change from the founder to the next generation and discuss the major cultural problems for leaders of second- and third-generation family firms.

The Dynamics of Change to Succeeding Generations

As discussed in Chapter Three, it appears to be the nature of family businesses to evolve into new and different cultural configurations. Some common conditions that trigger changes (and crises) in the family, the business, and the governing boards are:

1. The founder's death or serious illness.
2. The founder's retirement from active involvement in the business.
3. Merging with another company or selling a part of the business.

4. High growth or declining profitability.
5. Fundamental changes in the firm's domain—its products, markets, or the technologies used to make and distribute its goods and/or services.

These "triggering events" are all quite different, but each tends to have the same effect: moving the founder away from directly managing the business. In the case of death or illness, the founder's departure can be quite unexpected, leaving the firm and family in turmoil. Other founders plan for retirement and disengage slowly from the business. Merging or selling the business is another means of "letting go." When the business grows, declines, or changes direction, we often find that the founder's skills, which proved so useful at starting the business, now become a liability. Without adequate technical or managerial skills to adapt to a changing world, founders begin to flounder, and the aura of success surrounding them begins to crumble. When this occurs, the founder may be forced out by investors or family members who want to protect their investment. Other, more "enlightened" founders recognize their weaknesses and either step down willingly or bring in other managers with the skills that they lack. In any event, as the role of the founder begins to change, so does the firm's cultural configuration.

The founder's departure from active participation creates a power vacuum in the business and in the board that family and nonfamily members eagerly rush to fill. During the founder's rule, the power is concentrated in a single individual. When the founder departs, often a few family members and nonfamily managers form a sort of oligarchy, a dominant coalition that manages the business. In some cases, particularly in a crisis, a new, powerful leader emerges and creates a new vision for the organization. Such changes are generally not without major conflicts or power struggles.

Cultural Configurations
in the Second and Third Generations

The result of the transition dynamics is a new set of cultural configurations, often quite different from those created

by the founder. The family patterns frequently change from
patriarchal to conflicted. Some families do move into a collaborative mode, but this is clearly the exception. The board of directors usually becomes much more active once the founder is gone.
The diverse interests of the family or other investors create a
climate where the board either serves in an advisory capacity
or becomes the dominant force in guiding the business. Thus
the diversity of interests in the second generation creates various
"camps" and coalitions within the family and governing boards.

Each of the four business cultural patterns is also represented in succeeding generations.

The Paternalistic Culture. In some families, the paternalistic
tradition is carried on, usually by the oldest son. This pattern
was found in a large hotel chain that was initially torn with dissension. The oldest son of the founder, Fred, who eventually
succeeded his father, describes what happened:

> I think that the mistake that my father made.
> was that he said [to the children]: "You're equal
> owners, you really should share responsibility."
> What he should have said was, "When I go, Fred
> takes over." I tried, at first, to live this idea that
> you are all equal owners. But there were six people
> involved and ten different relationships. It worked
> all right for six months until one of my brothers
> decided that he had too many problems with his
> wife. She kept talking about things going on in the
> business and she didn't understand the business.
> This was making him too anxious and he asked if
> meetings could be held without her. There were also
> other problems. As long as Dad was there as the
> cement and everything was still theoretical, and
> there were no problems to deal with that would keep
> people awake at night, it worked fine. But later on
> [after Dad's death] rivalries began. Finally I said
> to each one of them, "I'm your father from now
> on" and everything has been fine since. I guess that
> the rest of the family, except for one member, be-

came more comfortable when I took over. One member that wasn't more comfortable sold her stock.

Other firms have followed this pattern, either because the founder designated a successor or because one family member emerged as the victor after considerable conflict. While this cultural pattern is relatively stable, because of the presence of a clear authority figure, it still retains the disadvantages of the paternalistic pattern described in Chapter Four.

The Laissez-Faire Culture. The laissez-faire pattern is also common in the second generation. This pattern typically emerges in three situations: (1) the family feels comfortable trusting non-family employees with significant responsibility; (2) the family is not very knowledgeable or competent in managing the business, so they turn over most of the management responsibility to trusted employees; or (3) second-generation family members lack the desire and commitment to carry on the traditions established by the founder; they are unwilling to make the kinds of sacrifices that the founder made in managing the business. The kind of laissez-faire management often found in the second generation is represented in companies such as National Cash Register, where Frederick Patterson (John Patterson's son) turned over much of the management responsibility to J. H. Barringer, and Levi Strauss & Co., where the Stern brothers became even more distant from the firm's activities.

The advantage of the laissez-faire pattern is its ability to reward and motivate nonfamily members, since they are given a great deal of freedom and autonomy. With this new freedom, company employees are often able to take the initiative to greatly expand the business. However, there are problems, too, primarily the lack of control over important functions and employees feeling that the family is abdicating its leadership responsibilities. In the case of Levi Strauss, for example, the family was able to expand operations greatly by allowing nonfamily employees to build and operate manufacturing facilities all over the world. However, because the family was not able to monitor the activities of all these plants, the quality of the product suffered in the 1970s.

The Participative Culture. The participative cultural pattern, rarely found in the first generation, begins to emerge in the second generation. In firms such as the Brown Corporation and Donnelly Corporation, the founders' sons eschewed the autocratic management styles of their fathers. Having experienced many of the stifling effects of the paternalistic pattern, the new leaders of the second generation seek to encourage collaboration. They often create committees, boards, and other forums to mediate their disputes.

The strength of the participative pattern is found in the way decisions are made. Because there is more input, decisions tend to be made at the point of the problem and better information is available to make those decisions. Also there tends to be a greater degree of commitment to carry out decisions when individuals can influence the decisions. Problems emerge from this pattern, however, when people begin to believe that all problems need to be handled participatively. This slows down decision making tremendously and can result in "decision paralysis"—no one is willing to risk making a decision unless they can get others to agree.

The Professional Culture. The professional cultural pattern is very common in family firms where the family wants to remove itself from management. Bringing in the "hired guns," as one founder put it, is sometimes seen as the solution to management succession. Some family firms, however, attempt to create a professional pattern by sending their sons and daughters away to business schools or other training grounds. This "professional" training has proven to be a source of conflict in some of the firms we studied. Typically, the founder, with little formal training, uses "seat of the pants" management. The college-trained children, having learned the "proper" way to manage a business, reject what they consider archaic business practices. Conflicts inevitably ensue; often the children become estranged from the family and the firm. In one family firm, for example, the son was sent to MIT to receive his formal training at the Sloan School of Management. After completing his degree, however, he found to his surprise that his new ideas were not valued by family members and he was quickly ostracized. He is now struggling to find a place for himself outside the family business. Since most successful family firms will encounter a number of problems associated with professional managers, Chapter Six will explore these issues in more detail.

Challenges for the Next Generations

Second- and third-generation leaders of family firms face many challenges. The success of future generations, and of the business itself, often depends on their ability to manage these common problems.

Avoiding the Rebecca Syndrome. Daphne du Maurier wrote a novel about a plain young woman who married a widower. She was constantly plagued by the comparisons between her and the first wife, Rebecca. In every instance, she failed to measure up to the ghost of the beautiful Rebecca. Second- and third-generation business leaders often have the same problem. They cannot shake the ghost of the founder. They feel constrained to follow tradition and are criticized by others who feel they have not lived up to expectations. The following two examples (names are fictional) illustrate this problem.

Larry Peppertine is running the family enterprises: a cattle ranch, a residential development business, and a restaurant. Larry's father turned everything over to him in excellent condition. Larry's brothers went into different occupations, where they are very successful. Larry felt that someone in the family should take over from their father. Larry has a college education, is intelligent, and has held many leadership positions in the community. However, things have not gone well for him. He is constantly being criticized by family members for the way he has "ruined" the business. Larry himself admits, "Dad is constantly telling me that I am going to lose everything he built up." He also admits that he didn't *really* want to get into the business. If he weren't too old, he would make a career change. The family doesn't appreciate his hard work anyway (Checketts, 1985, p. 1).

David Bluebird's father died unexpectedly of a stroke. At the time David had been working in the family business for only a short period. David's father had started the business in the middle of the Depression; by the time he died, it was worth several million dollars. Mack Bluebird had gained a reputation as a shrewd, hard-driving businessman and he wanted his son to follow in his footsteps. After his father's death, David faced a personal crisis. He found that he couldn't handle living with his father's ghost. The employees had worked for Mack for many years and were very loyal to him. Whenever a decision was to be made, the employees consulted the founder's ghost. "What do you think your father would do?" they would ask David. When David made a decision the employees didn't like, they would remind him, "your father wouldn't have done it this way." The word around the office, the town, and the industry was that David was going to ruin the business. David became angry and bitter. He hadn't asked for the job, or for his father to die so soon. To sort out these problems David sought out professional counseling. After three years, David's therapist convinced him that the business was *his*—not his father's—and he should run the business as he saw fit. Armed with this insight, David began to expand the business at an incredible rate. Now he is no longer seen as "Mack's son," but is referred to as "David—a shrewd businessman" (Checketts, 1985, p. 3).

These two cases illustrate how differently the Rebecca Syndrome was handled. In the first case, Larry became bitter and defeated. He should have clarified his own feelings about a career in the family business before accepting the job. He also needed to clarify expectations that his father and other family members had about his role in the business. In the second case, David realized he had a serious personal problem in dealing with the legacy of his father. By recognizing the problem and finding a competent therapist, he was able actively to confront and debunk the Rebecca myth and eventually became a successful leader.

"Pruning" the Culture. Second- and third-generation leaders have the unique opportunity to reevaluate the artifacts, perspectives, values, and assumptions of prior regimes. The successful leaders in future generations are able to "prune" the cultural pattern—eliminating outdated practices, preserving useful values, and grafting in new ideas and practices that will help the

firm adapt to its environment (Wilkins and Patterson, 1985).
For example, in the Brown Corporation, John Brown, Jr., when
he took over for his father, realized that the culture needed to
change in certain ways. The business had almost 500 employees—
too large for one man to manage. So he began to delegate responsibility and foster participation. But he didn't change the
culture entirely. John, Sr.'s values of "innovation" and "taking
care of the company employees" were still continued. Although
some of the means of carrying out those values had changed
under John, Jr.'s leadership, the ends remained the same. Rather
than destroying all that the founder has created—as so often
happens when the firm goes through crisis and change—succeeding generations should attempt to build upon previous competen-
cies and values that are still useful, while modifying other aspects
of the culture. In doing this, however, the leaders must remember that culture is a *pattern* and that a change in one core assumption may alter the entire culture. "Cultural pruning" must
be done with great care.

A Time of Conflicts

Family conflicts also begin to emerge during these transition periods. Often latent conflicts that had been suppressed
for years come out into the open. The founder created a common vision for the firm and family, but after his departure the
diversity of interests and values within the family comes to light.
We will look at some situations that often seem to present problems, and then highlight several techniques for solving them.

Some of the more common issues around which these conflicts occur are:

How Should the Company's Assets Be Used? Some family
members, generally those not in the business, will feel that the
firm's profits should be distributed to them as shareholders.
Others, however, believe that the profits should be poured back
into the business so it can grow and thrive. This is probably
the most common issue that triggers family conflicts.

Will the Assets Be Shared Equitably? The problem of "equity"
is another common issue for family members and nonfamily

members alike. Brothers, sisters, in-laws, the founder's spouse, and other members of the extended family often have different views of what is equitable. Nonfamily members believe that they should be rewarded for their contributions to the business. Some of the most serious and bitter schisms occur within a family firm when people feel they have not received equal treatment.

How Should Decisions Be Made? Under the watchful eye of the founder, family members had little input into the firm's decision making. Now, without this guidance, family members and nonfamily managers must create new mechanisms to handle decisions. Some family members, usually the founder's spouse or oldest son, may feel that they should assume the role of decision maker. Other, less powerful family members tend to argue for more collaboration in the decision-making process. Whether to go public, who to hire, what strategy to follow—these are all decisions that family members want to influence. Differences about the method of decision making prove to be fertile ground for family squabbles.

Who Is the Family? This question concerns who is entitled to the benefits of family ownership. Some family members, on the basis of a variety of criteria—age, sex, relationship with the founder, competence, education—may be precluded from becoming significant shareholders or reaching top management positions. The status of in-laws often changes in the second generation, as they seek an expanded role in the firm. The question of who is "in" and who is "out" is of utmost importance to those in the family business. A great deal of conflict occurs as status changes and new roles are created in the second generation.

Dealing with Conflict

The diverse interests and conflicts that we see in second- and third-generation family firms are often the central problems around which many other problems revolve. Such conflicts may lead to irreconcilable differences that damage both family and firm. Younger brothers or sisters do not want to be subservient to their older siblings, or they feel that the firm is moving in the wrong direction. Others may feel that they are not being treated fairly. When such schisms occur, families respond in several ways. Some families create a council or committee, representing the various groups, to handle their disputes. Unfortunately, these councils, rather than solving the problems, often become the battlegrounds where little gets accomplished. This is not because the idea itself is bad, but because family members have not learned how to manage their conflicts with one another.

A second option often used is the appointment of a "caretaker" president or chief executive officer. The caretaker, often a nonfamily member, is chosen when no one family member can muster enough support. Because they are compromise candidates whom all family members can generally endorse but for whom there is little enthusiasm, caretakers generally find themselves in the eye of a hurricane with little power and support. Appointing a caretaker usually just delays the conflict, but that delay can be helpful if in the meantime conflicts can be resolved or a successor groomed who has widespread support.

A third option is to admit that the conflicts probably cannot be managed and then break up various segments of the business into new and distinct organizational entities. The theory behind this approach is that separating the warring factions removes the source of the conflict. A number of family firms have tried this option, with mixed results.

Using a Mediator

Family members, board members, family consultants, and nonfamily managers may find themselves in the role of mediator during these transition periods. In some family firms, the spouse of the founder plays this crucial role. They can see the differing points of view and can determine where there are common interests. Because they are seen as impartial and working for the good of all family members, spouses can have considerable influence in settling disputes. They often have a significant ownership position as well, and this also gives them a great deal of power during these transition periods.

The family lawyer, banker, or consultant may also assume the role of mediator. In the case of the Brown Corporation, the family banker helped mediate the many conflicts between father and son. In another family firm, the family relied on the advice and help of two trusted consultants to help the founder, his wife, and his children manage many of the personal and interpersonal conflicts they encountered as they grappled with the problem of succession.

In other organizations such as Steinberg, Inc., Jack Levine, Sam Steinberg's trusted adviser, assumed the presidency after Sam died. Levine emerged as the leader of the organization largely on the basis of management acumen and his ability to work with the Steinberg family. He understood many of the conflicts, strengths, and weaknesses in the family and was able to both manage the firm and "manage" the family during his tenure as president. Such mediators play a critical but often overlooked role during the transitions that take place across generations.

Conflict Management Tools

In addition to the general approaches to solving conflicts that we have already discussed, there are some specific techniques that can be useful.

Asset Management Board. This can be a useful vehicle to air disputes and train family members (Beckhard and Dyer, 1983a). Such a board, which is separate from the board of directors, is composed of key family members who take up issues such as succession planning, stock distribution, training and development of family members, and so on. Outside consultants or key nonfamily executives may be brought into this group to facilitate the discussion or to provide useful information. Such a board can work to create a collective vision of the future if there is a climate of trust rather than defensiveness among family members. To do this often requires the use of a consultant skilled at facilitating conflicts and handling sensitive issues that might "blow up" if the family were to attempt to manage them alone.

Third Party. This approach to managing conflict requires family members to be willing to negotiate with one another to iron out their differences (Walton, 1969). A third party acts as a mediator to reduce defensiveness, outline the issues on which the parties differ, and to see that the parties reach some agreement, generally in writing, that they all commit to follow. This has been used successfully to manage both interpersonal and intergroup conflicts.

Role Negotiation. This technique may be needed when there is significant ambiguity about roles and expectations. Family and nonfamily members may experience significant stress and conflicts about their roles after the founder is gone. Managing these conflicts requires family members (and nonfamily employees, when necessary) to meet together to share expectations about one another's roles in the business, in the family, and on the board of directors. A facilitator might be needed to clarify what is said in such a session, to get the participants to understand one another's roles, and, if necessary, to develop action plans to change behaviors and expectations.

Confrontation Meeting. This approach can be used to gather organizationwide data about serious problems and conflicts (Beckhard, 1967). The process involves getting together the key people who have data about a particular problem and having them share and confront that data with the group. Problems are then identified and action plans developed. A confrontation meeting generally requires a consultant. The participants have to be willing to share and explore data about themselves and others. Trust, openness, and the ability to handle negative feedback without becoming overly defensive are essential for this intervention to work effectively.

The conflict management interventions mentioned above can and have been used to manage some of the conflicts facing family firms. It is important to remember, however, that while these mechanisms are helpful to identify the issues and attempt to manage them, without a shared vision or goal, getting family members to consent to work out their differences can be very difficult.

Families in Conflict: Two Case Histories

Dunckley Music. Dunckley Music was founded in the late 1940s by Willis R. Dunckley, who got into the retail music business after ordering a number of used pianos and other musical instruments (Brown, 1985a). He started a successful music store in Ogden, Utah, and eventually brought his brother, William, into the business. Although the business continued to thrive, the brothers realized that the one store could not support two growing families, so William left to open his own music store in a neighboring state.

As time went on, the music business became more competitive, so Willis Dunckley loaded a truck with pianos and other musical instruments and began selling them on the road. This "traveling store" proved to be very successful; in fact it became the hallmark of Dunckley Music. Willis had four sons, Robert, Richard, John, and Ralph; as teenagers, all had worked part-time in the business. Robert, the oldest son, decided that he wanted a career in the business. His attempt was not very satisfying, however, because he was not as aggressive as his father; he soon left the business. In the early 1970s, the second son, Richard, became disenchanted with his career as a schoolteacher and came to work for his father, although he had little knowledge of the business. Shortly after, Willis suffered a debilitating stroke and was forced to retire. Quite unexpectedly, Richard was thrust into the founder's role. Six months after Richard took over, the fourth son, Ralph, who had just graduated from college with a business degree, was invited to join the business. Pooling their efforts, Richard and Ralph were able to operate a successful music store. Because of this initial success, the sons decided to expand operations to other communities and invited the other two brothers to join them. Thus all four sons began operating stores or warehouses in different locations.

As they began working together, however, some of the brothers began to feel that they were not being treated equitably. Some stores were more profitable than others. So they decided to divide the locations and give each brother ownership of his part of the business, while retaining the family name on the stores. There was little coordination between the brothers, and in one instance two found themselves competing against one another.

Robert was given the firm's warehouse, which he eventually lost because of mismanagement. John built a store in the same area as the original store, but it has not been very profitable. Richard has lost a great deal of market share in his stores, and was forced to sell one store and close another. Ralph operated the original store, which has remained profitable, but has had to close two others. Intense competition has made it difficult for the brothers' stores to survive as independent entities. In recent months the brothers have enlisted the help of consultants and have tried to collaborate on developing a common product line and advertising strategy. Their efforts, however, have not been very successful because the brothers still are unable to see the advantages of pooling their resources.

Working together, the brothers, even though relatively inexperienced, were able to develop some synergy: they could compensate for one another's weaknesses, and cooperatively market and advertise their products. Standing alone, they have not been as successful. Rather than one strong, integrated business, the brothers have created a number of weak businesses.

We are not suggesting that dividing up a family business into separate units never makes sense; in some cases, dividing the business proves successful. In this case, however, and in some others, the firm was divided along lines that made little business sense, although the division did serve to assuage the feelings of the brothers. Under such conditions, the business generally declines.

The Nebeker Family. One family that has attempted to use a third party to mediate their disputes is the Nebeker family (fictional names), owners of a number of retail stores (Peay, 1985). The cultural pattern of the Nebeker business is paternalistic, with Ellis Nebeker running the entire business at age seventy-three. His one son in the business, Norman, has had little influence on his father, who makes all the important decisions. The family is highly conflicted; Norman and Ellis frequently fight about their roles and responsibilities. Ellis's wife often takes sides with Norman, while Norman's older brother, Bill, who does not work in the business but is an interested shareholder, generally agrees with his father. The relationship between the two brothers is cool at best. There is a board of directors, but it is a paper board with no influence; it has met only once since it was created several years ago. In this cultural configuration, no one has been able to play the role of mediator.

As conflict between Ellis and Norman escalated, and Norman threatened to leave the business and take his wife and Ellis's only grandchildren with him, the family decided that they needed a third party to help them with their conflicts. Through an office of the Small Business Administration they located a consultant, trained in both therapy and organizational development, to help them.

During the consultant's initial meeting with the family, all the problems described above were manifest. Norman accused his father of a number of misdeeds; Ellis was very defensive and attacked Norman. The mother supported Norman; the brother sided with Ellis. After this meeting, the consultant decided to meet with each family member individually to get their "story" and to develop a plan of action. After interviewing the family, the consultant believed that the basic problem was the lack of clear goals and roles.

At the next meeting with the family, the consultant helped the Nebekers to analyze the sources of the conflicts. Three major agreements were reached:

1. The family wanted the business to continue as a family-owned enterprise. They did not want to sell the business or bring in outside management.
2. Each family member agreed that Ellis should begin to move away from active operation of the business.
3. Norman was the candidate most prepared to succeed his father.

The consultant then helped the family make specific plans to carry out these goals. Ellis was to spend less time at the office and delegate more responsibility. Norman was to have more authority but counsel with Ellis on major decisions.

The results of this intervention have been mixed. For a short period, both Ellis and Norman followed the plan outlined by the consultant. Relations between them improved; so did the functioning of the business. Over time, however, Ellis began to take over more and more control of the business—in violation of the agreement—and he and Norman have had some heated arguments. They still have not learned how to manage their conflicts without some outside assistance.

The case of the Nebekers illustrates how third parties can be used to help manage conflict. The consultant was successful in helping the family in the short run. However, unless the family is committed to the change and continually works on the problems, success is likely to be short-lived.

Creating a Collective Vision

The founder of a family firm is faced with the fundamental problem of creating a business that will survive. Along with this comes the creation of a vision or philosophy that will give employees and the company direction. In the second generation and later, the problem changes somewhat. Because of the bifurcation of interests that occurs in succeeding generations, the business and family often find themselves wandering without direction, moving from crisis to crisis, conflict to conflict, without any overriding strategy or goals. Thus the challenge for leaders of future generations is to bring together diverse interests and coalitions. This requires the leaders to articulate clearly a vision of the future and to show various family members and interest groups how their needs will be met under the new regime. The sacrifices that must be made for the good of the group need to be spelled out and a plan of action created. This does not mean that conflicts should be ignored, for mediating conflicts is critical, but articulating a vision of a shared future is the vital first step.

Six

Cultural Ramifications
of Public Ownership
and Professional Management

As one studies the histories of highly successful family firms, the inexorable movement to public ownership and professional management is all too apparent. This trend has been described by other writers such as Berle and Means (1968), Galbraith (1971), and Chandler (1977), so we will not discuss it in detail here. The focus of this chapter will be on the impact of public ownership and professional management on the culture of family firms.

Even though the actual number of family businesses that go public is very small, founders or other family leaders often agonize over this decision. The question of bringing in professional managers is more common, but just as difficult. Because they have never gone through such transitions, leaders of family firms frequently fail to understand the full implications of these major decisions. By studying firms that have gone through such transitions, however, we have learned some of the problems, tradeoffs, and dilemmas that often accompany these changes. This chapter will describe the impact of public ownership and professional management on the cultures of family firms and suggest some issues to be managed for those who are contemplating these options.

The Decision to Go Public

Our studies and others have indicated that many forces can drive members of family firms to offer company stock for public consumption (Salomon, 1977). We can summarize these "driving forces" into eight common reasons.

1. To Increase Personal Wealth. To some leaders of family firms, increasing personal or family wealth was the primary motive behind the decision to go public. Much of the founder's wealth was tied up in the business, and a public offering provided the means to get some of that money out of the business. The founder of a computer software company noted that until he took his company public, he was a rich man only "on paper," and that he felt compelled to sell most of the company stock to a large conglomerate to receive the monetary rewards of his work.

2. To Diversify. Some founders felt that by owning a family business they had "all their eggs in one basket." A public offering allowed them to diversify their holdings, thereby lowering the overall risk of their investments. In a few cases, the ultimate goal of the founders was to sell the business so they could move on to other investments. These "deal makers" rarely stayed with one business or investment too long. Creating a business—not building one—seemed to be their primary motivation.

3. To Obtain Equity Capital for Expansion. In many cases the need for equity capital to finance expansion was the driving force behind the decision to go public. The rapidly growing companies always seemed to be cash short and their founders often disdained debt. Sale of company stock was the most viable option.

4. To Attract and Motivate Employees. Another reason behind a public stock offering was to attract and motivate company executives. The use of stock and stock options as rewards for employees was seen as a powerful enticement by family and nonfamily executives alike. Other founders felt it was their obligation to "share the wealth" with their employees, and going public allowed them to do this.

5. To Avoid IRS Valuation of Company Assets. When the founder of a private company dies, the Internal Revenue Service will determine the value of the company for inheritance taxes (in the absence of a public market for stock, which would automatically be the value). To avoid such IRS determinations (founders seem to distrust the IRS), going public is often seen as the best option. For example, in the case of the Brown Corporation, John Brown, Sr.'s serious illness in the late 1940s forced him to think seriously about the tax burden on his family if he had died. He decided that the family would be better off if the value of the company was determined by the market—not the IRS.

6. *To Satisfy Investment Bankers.* Founders are often barraged by investment bankers urging them to go public. The investment bankers often argue that the family could go public with their stock, reap the financial advantages of such an offering, and still remain in control of the company. Thus the constant prodding from the financial community is another force pushing the founder to go public.

7. *To "Professionalize" Management.* In a few cases going public was a sign that the family was no longer going to dominate the management of the company. Going public means that outside board members are brought in. This enables the family to gain outside expertise and demonstrate that the business is not merely a family enterprise. It is also a way to avoid or mitigate against nepotism, because it signals to the business community that there are opportunities for nonfamily members as well.

8. *To Sell Out.* Going public is also the means of getting out of the family business. In a few cases, going public was seen as the major step in moving family involvement out of the business.

The Unintended Consequences of Public Ownership

There are a number of "good" reasons for taking a family business public, but there are also some consequences—not all of them positive. To illustrate some of the effects of going public, we will turn to one example—Richard Salomon, the former owner of Charles of the Ritz, a small cosmetics company with a chain of hair salons (Salomon, 1977). Salomon's story represents some of the dynamics of public ownership found in other family firms we studied.

Salomon had a number of reasons for going public: to increase wealth, to avoid IRS determination of company value, to gain equity to expand, and to reward executives. However, a number of unforeseen events occurred.

Conflict Among Executives and Family Members. When the announcement was made that the company was going public, relationships among his top executives began to fray. They started to worry about how many shares each was going to get as they jockeyed for favored positions. Salomon reports: "Men with whom I had never exchanged an unpleasant word over compensation or perquisites became snarling tigers when it came to asserting their claims to a large allotment of shares" (1977, p. 127). Overcoming such jealousy and bitterness became the central issue for the management team, and it took a great deal of energy away from the operations of the business. In many family firms similar conflicts also occur among family members vying for company ownership, although in Salomon's case this was not a major problem since his children were still quite young at the time.

Focus on Short-Run Results. Another new source of concern is the price of the company's stock. Once the stock goes public, maintaining or increasing its price becomes a chief concern of management. In the past, Salomon had had the luxury of developing plans that would ensure the long-term viability of the company. However, with the advent of public ownership, the top-management team at Charles of the Ritz began to focus on short-term actions that had immediate impact on the stock price. As Salomon put it: "We began to run scared with one eye on short term results" (p. 128). Salomon also began to worry that company employees, friends, and other investors might lose money after investing in the firm's stock. This became an obsession with him, and it influenced him to emphasize results in the short run, sometimes at the expense of long-term growth and stability. This concern for investors was also true of other family businesses such as Levi Strauss & Co. The Haas family actually reimbursed employees who lost money on their stock during the recession of the early 1970s, for the family felt obligated to protect their employees' investment in the company.

Resentment of Public Scrutiny. One of the more onerous bur-
dens placed on leaders by public ownership is public review of
their actions. Outside stockholders and board members become
intensely interested in the affairs of the firm, and the founder
and the family are now under the obligation to make public what
had long been held secret. Salomon found he was beginning
to protect himself and his decisions from those "Monday morning quarterbacks" who were now able to review and criticize
his judgment. With the various review processes in a public company, decision making begins to slow down, and the entrepreneurial spirit of the founder and the company may begin to
wane.

Change in Power Structure. A change in ownership necessarily
means a change in the way power is distributed. Ownership is
the major power base in the family business. In most cases we
studied, public ownership significantly diluted the power and
influence of the founder and the family in a relatively short period
of time, usually within five years. Such changes in the firm's
power structure often lead to major changes in the culture of
the firm, the governing boards, and at times even the family—
particularly if family members have divergent views on how the
stock is to be distributed and how (or if) dividends are to be
paid. Future opportunities for power and influence in the business by family members may also be stymied or cut off with
a move to public ownership. Nepotism is much more difficult
to maintain when one must answer to shareholders.

Risk of Takeover. Finally, issuing stock to the public makes
the company more susceptible to a takeover bid. Charles of the
Ritz was eventually acquired by Squibb in 1971. Although this
was a friendly takeover, Salomon suddenly found himself working for another company. Such a situation is anathema to the
vast majority of founders and entrepreneurs. After realizing that
he could not work for someone else and have his performance
reviewed, Salomon decided to retire gracefully from active participation and found himself in the role of a board member and
consultant. Other entrepreneurs we studied who had "sold out"
were much like Salomon. They would frequently visit their company, see all the problems that the company was embroiled in,
and then feel powerless to do anything about it since they no

longer had any formal authority. Such situations are excruciatingly painful for those powerless founders who see their companies faltering or moving in directions that they believe are unwise.

Public Ownership and Culture Change

These examples have illustrated that going public frequently changes the culture of the family firm. Top management feels compelled to focus on short-run results. Keeping one eye on the stock price changes the orientation from the future—investing in long-run returns—to managing the problems of the present. Relationships also tend to become more individualistic and competitive. The result is increased conflict in the family and the business. Outside review by stockholders or board members forces the family to consult with other parties before making any decision. The family can no longer act with complete independence. Traditional family practices such as nepotism often cannot survive in a publicly owned company.

Professional Management in the Family Firm

The recruitment of professional management into a family firm is often tied to the problem of going public. In many cases we studied, the two coincided. The two usual reasons for bringing in professionals are, first, that the family lacks the necessary management or technical expertise to continue to run the business effectively; and, second, professional management is often seen as the "rational" alternative to nepotism and familial conflicts that plague a family business. One consultant to family businesses has even gone so far as to suggest: "In general the wisest course for any business, family or nonfamily, is to move to professional management as quickly as possible" (Levinson, 1971, p. 98).

However, bringing in professional management, like going public, clearly presents some tradeoffs and problems. We will briefly discuss some of these tradeoffs and then present three case studies to illustrate the impact of professional management on a family business.

Characteristics of Professional Management

The introduction of professional management into a family business often leads to profound changes in the structure and function of these businesses. We will outline four of the more significant areas of change.

New Leadership Patterns. New leadership styles emerge with the introduction of professional management, because of the very nature of "professional manager." The first major difference between professional and family managers has to do with their backgrounds and training. The professional managers generally have had some formal business training, often an M.B.A. degree. They pride themselves in their knowledge of finance, accounting, marketing, or other business skills. They often have different personal backgrounds than the other employees. For example, in the case of the Brown Corporation, the professional managers were generally younger than the indigenous work force; they came from urban centers and had worked at large, publicly owned companies. Founders of family enterprises often come from rather poor circumstances, have little formal training, and believe that they had to "pull themselves up by their bootstraps" to succeed. Such differences can bring conflict between the professionals and those who have known only management by the family.

There are also significant differences in what have been termed "motivational, analytical, and interpersonal" orientations (Schein, 1983). Founders are motivated to create an organization while taking significant risks. Professional managers are the overseers, the caretakers, who attempt to build on what the founders have created. Founders often have a deep commitment to the enterprise; professional managers often seem to be more concerned about their own careers. This feeling was displayed in an interview with a high-level professional manager at the Brown Corporation: "As long as I'm challenged, I'm here. But I think that somewhere along the line I'm going to come up to a block somewhere. . . . I'm thirty-five years old—where am I going to go? . . . Once you get to a certain level, there's nothing more; *there's nothing more!* The question is, do I settle down and retire here, and say, 'Well, I've got a pretty good job and a nice house.' . . . But somewhere along the line, two, three, four, five years from now if I'm still doing [what I'm doing] I know I'm going to be bored and if I'm bored I'm gone'' (Dyer, 1984a, p. 122).

Most professional managers are committed to a business only if the job is "challenging" and there is the possibility for advancement. In the absence of either, they quickly begin looking for another job. This particular manager did become "bored" with the Brown Corporation and left the company two years after making this statement.

The interpersonal and analytical orientations of professional managers and founders are often at odds. Professional managers tend to follow "professional" codes of conduct to guide their behavior. They are often seen as impersonal, prone to using bureaucratic rules to enforce their policies. In contrast, the founders are often seen as "charismatic father figures" who have developed what employees see as a close relationship to them. They also act quickly, often relying on intuition or experience to make decisions.

Alfred Chandler (1962) noted these differences in his description of Billy Durant, the founder of General Motors, and his successor, the professional manager Alfred P. Sloan: "The difference between the approaches of the two men to the problem of administration, reflects contrasting personalities, education, and experience. Durant was a small, lively, warm man. Nearly everyone called him Billy. Mr. Sloan was tall, quiet, and cool. Increasing deafness heightened his reserve. Nearly everyone called him Mr. Sloan, even his closest associates. Where Durant's initial achievements have been in marketing, Sloan's were in production. To Durant, this builder of empires, the details of organization seemed unimportant. But to Alfred Sloan, this lack of attention seemed inexcusable; his rational precise mind found the promoter's ways of operation wasteful, inefficient, and dangerous" (p. 130).

Such differences in background, personality, and leadership styles often lead to major changes in the nature of the family business after professional management begins to enter the firm.

New Psychological Contract Between Management and Workers.
We also find that the nature of the psychological contract—
that is, the perceived relationship between employer and
employee that determines the conditions of employment—often
changes with the introduction of professional management. In
the family-owned firm, the relationship between employee and
owner is often familial. The founder and his family "take care
of" the workers, and in return the family receives the employees'
loyalty and dedication. In many cases people join the business
because they are committed to the "cause" of the founder. The
"contract" is based on a personal relationship with the founder,
and this relationship may extend beyond the walls of the business
to the community as well. Family firms often support emergency
welfare funds, athletic teams, company picnics, choirs, and other
activities that serve as the center of the social activities for the
employees and the community at large.

In contrast, the psychological contract between professional managers and workers is often utilitarian in nature. Employees see their commitment and involvement in the firm as
a function of their salary, bonuses, and other fringe benefits.
Employees expect monetary rewards or other tangible benefits
in return for their performance and commitment to the business.
Relationships become more impersonal, strictly employer-em-
ployee, without the familial tone of other cultural patterns. This
new, utilitarian contract tends to put increased distance among
workers, management, and those family members still in the
business. Such "distancing" is illustrated in another story from
the Brown Corporation, told by a company old-timer (Dyer,
1984a, p. 126):

> John, Sr., used to be out in the plant. He
> used to know everyone by name. There was a great
> sense of camaraderie that was possible with a small
> organization. . . . In our organization the president
> or chairman of the board used to present guys with
> a five-year award—a pin—and after ten years all
> they do is change the number and so on. . . . The
> sad part of it is that [the company with new manage-

ment] has gotten way from [this tradition] as we have changed the name of the game. It is no longer a Brown tradition in the sense of having a Brown family member present the pin. Now a division manager does it for the five year award and for the ten year it is the general manager. Reed Larson [the president] gets involved at fifteen years. It takes away the personal thing and the older folks that are retiring now remember that. When I give an award now and talk to the people, one of the first things they do is go into their tool box and bring out the old pictures [with John, Sr., when he gave them their pins] and say, "I don't know if you remember. . . ." We are getting more and more people when the time for a service award comes saying, "just send me the pin. I don't want my picture taken." . . . In the past they looked forward to it. They would keep it and that is the first thing they would drag out [and show me] [Dyer, 1984a, p. 126].

Organization-Community Relations. The founders and families we studied were intensely interested in the well-being of the communities that were the host for their organizations. They were often found on the chamber of commerce, school boards, charity fund-raising committees, and numerous other activities designed to strengthen the community. Our studies and a recent study conducted by Christopher Meek in the Jamestown area of New York State suggest that the nature of the relationship between the organization and the community often changes as families sell stock to the public, sell out, or turn over operations to professional managers.

Where there are "absentee" owners with professional managers, the needs and concerns of the local community tend to be less of a factor in decision making. Decisions about layoffs or plant closings are orchestrated by individuals with few social ties to the community. The social impact of any decision is less relevant than the economic consequences for the firm. In many of the cases we studied, one of the first acts of the professional managers was to lay off or fire a number of long-term employees. This invariably incited negative feelings toward the company by the community and embarrassed the owning family. However, the professionals, who did not see their careers as being tied to their standing in the community, would argue that company effectiveness, or even survival, should be the paramount goal. In the Brown Corporation, many professional managers felt ill at ease living in the community because of some of their actions. They preferred to live in outlying areas and commute to work. This caused widespread resentment among the local employees and those in the community. One employee said, "We don't have near as many people that live here and expect their kids to go to school here. Upper-level people that come in have not chosen to live in Orangeville. They go somewhere else" (Dyer, 1984a, p. 127).

Another employee commented: "In the old days we knew most everybody. I think most everybody lived in Orangeville. New people usually lived in Orangeville. They are getting away from that now as far as the officers are concerned. I understand that because I think it is probably easier to live where you are not part of the community in case you have to fire somebody or when bad things happen. When there are recessions it must be hard for the managers to live in the village. Then, too, they should be supporting the village with their taxes. They used to be very involved. John, Jr., was president of the school board for a long long time. . . . I think that people who work here should be involved" (Dyer, 1984a, p. 128).

The lack of community involvement by professional management tends to be fostered by their career orientation. They view themselves as "managers"; they are oriented toward climbing the corporate ladder. The employees who "grew up" under the leadership of the founder often see themselves as "company men and women," dedicated to the company and the community. This change in company-community relations is often an unintended consequence of moving to professional management.

Organizational Effectiveness. Finally, there is the impact of professional management on organizational effectiveness. As professional managers enter a family business, they tend to use shorter time horizons and focus on "getting the numbers." Because many professional managers enter a family business during a crisis period, they feel great pressure to get quick results and turn the company around. Decisions are often made to fire or lay off employees or to sell parts of the business that are not profitable. They are less concerned with product development and innovation and devote most of their energy to improving the company's financial picture. In one family-owned business the vice-president of engineering noted that since professional managers had taken over the business, he has had great difficulty getting funds for basic research. The innovation-oriented founder of the company often encouraged such research. But there had not been a significant new product developed since the professional managers entered the company in large numbers eight years earlier.

Professional managers are more likely to try to encourage company growth and use company profits to enhance the company and their careers. Family members may wish to use these funds for themselves or others in the family. Such a conflict in goals makes formulating coherent policies difficult. All too often we hear of professional managers hired to turn a company around—which they did—only to be fired when they discover that the family's goals and aspirations for the business and its profits are different from their own. In other cases, the family may be forced by other investors to live by the professional managers' rules.

We have also discovered that there tends to be higher turnover and job dissatisfaction as professional managers attempt to change the culture of a family business. Increase in union activity is common. Meek (1985) discovered that firms controlled by professional management and absentee owners had more strikes and longer strikes than businesses that continued to be operated by the family. Other studies have shown that leaders of family firms are much more concerned about strikes and other union activity than their professional counterparts.

Professional Management and Culture Change

These examples illustrate fundamental culture changes that often occur when a family business makes the transition to professional management. In Chapter Two we examined some of the more common cultural patterns found in family firms and found they were often highly paternalistic. The "professional" cultural pattern, also described in Chapter Two, is based on universalistic or competence-related assumptions with a strong emphasis on individual achievement and advancement. Thus the "professional" culture often represents a marked departure from the symbols, traditions, beliefs, and values that were held by founders and their families. Indeed, professional managers often view it as their "duty" to eradicate the "archaic" practices of the past. One professional manager in the Brown Corporation described his initial reaction to the "Brown culture" this way:

> Many people really took it very hard when I came in as a marketing manager. Within about a year or so, most of the employees I had to transfer or let go. They took this extremely hard because all these people were in their jobs 15 or 20 years and the new path was completely different. Most of the people I had in there I didn't need. . . . So that was a shock to a close family. I say "close family" because the problems are closely held. Everybody went out and got drunk together, and everybody closed the place down at the opening of deer [hunting] season. Of course, when you come in as an outsider you tend to see that as being inefficient. . . . You have to come in and kill some of these old sacred cows. Like I said, taking the first day of deer season—*that* was a sacred cow. . . . There was a time I really went through some hard times here trying to change some of those sacred cows [Dyer, 1984a, pp. 120–121].

Attempting to change "sacred cows" is a common experience when a professional manager enters a family business.

While such attempts may be "rational" and may in many cases improve the effectiveness of the business, significant conflicts and major cultural changes are often the result.

Changes in the culture of the board of directors and the family may also change. Professional managers frequently make their way onto the board of directors, while holding views and values different from those of the family. The move to professional management may also preclude family members from joining or advancing in the business. This may create significant conflicts between the professional management and the family, and among family members themselves, who may have different perspectives on the nature and degree of involvement by professional management.

The "Professionalization" of Family Firms: Three Case Studies

To illustrate the profound impact of profesional management on the cultures of family firms, we will present three short case histories. The first describes how new managers instigated a cultural revolution in the firm. The second depicts a family business that the founders believe was almost destroyed by professional management. The final case demonstrates how professional managers are forced to mediate between warring factions in the family business.

Bennett Enterprises. The Bennett Paint and Glass Company was founded in 1900 by John F. Bennett, the son of poor English immigrants to Utah. The Bennett family was financially insecure during John's early years, and to support his handicapped father and his mother, John went to work at age thirteen. He eventually became a bookkeeper in a prominent local company. In 1887 he accepted a partnership in a furniture company, but the business faltered and John lost 80 percent of his savings. Ten years later, in 1897, he and a few limited partners bought a failing paint and glass company. The partners named John president and the company immediately began to prosper. By 1900 the company's net worth was $102,000, and John changed the name to the Bennett Paint and Glass Company.

John Bennett was fanatically devoted to his business, working between ten and fourteen hours a day. He even kept his bride waiting at the altar for two hours when he found that he had too much work to do at the office. After the ceremony he dropped his wife off at their new home and quickly returned to work. On a personal level John was rather reserved; he never engaged in open displays of affection with his wife and children. He had what he called a "pragmatic" political philosophy—he described himself as a "Democratic, Republican, Roman Catholic, Socialist Mormon."

The culture of Bennett Paint and Glass was paternalistic. Employees said the company was "one large family" with John Bennett as the father figure. Few people were fired and the company avoided layoffs. During the Depression of the 1930s employee salaries were cut in an attempt to avoid layoffs.

The Bennett family was deeply involved in both the ownership and management of the business. John Bennett's brothers and sisters all had a stake in the business, and this brought significant conflicts that led to major schisms in the family. By 1930 John Bennett had either bought out or sold off parts of the company to his brothers and sisters, but he continued to have his three sons and two daughters involved in the company's affairs. After John's death in 1938, his oldest son, Wallace, took over; he continued many of the family traditions and greatly expanded the business. Then in 1950 Wallace was elected U.S. senator, and served in the Senate until 1974. During that time Wallace's brother Richard ran the business. Richard died unexpectedly in 1976, and control of the paint and glass business fell to Wally Bennett, Wallace's son.

At that point the company's stock was held in a family trust entitled the Bennett Association. More than 200 family members owned stock in the trust, but the authority for operating the trust and the business rested in the board of trustees, composed of Wallace Bennett, Wallace's brother Harold, nephews Richard K. Winters and Kenneth Smith, and nephew-in-law Donald Penny. The voting, however, was not distributed equally; the senator had two votes, Harold two, and the others one each. Thus Wallace and Harold, who generally agreed with one another, were able to control the board.

By 1981 things were not going well for the company. In 1976 the company experienced its first loss in many years, and the company continued to lose money for the next four years. In 1981 the anticipated loss was $3.2 million on revenues of $28 million. To find out what was wrong, the board commissioned Arthur Young & Co. to do a study of the business. Michael Silva was the chief consultant on the project. Silva, who had worked previously as an assistant to the president at Skaggs Foods, a corporate planner for a bank in Hawaii, and a consultant for Peat, Marwick, Mitchell & Co.'s bank consulting group, suggested that the position of chief executive officer be created to oversee the paint company and the other Bennett-owned businesses. Senator Bennett agreed, and in the search for a CEO the board decided to hire Silva to carry out the plan he had recommended. Silva initially took the job with two understandings. First, he would not have to go to the board for approval of his decisions. The board could fire him, but they couldn't overturn his decisions. Second, family members would be "protected" as much as possible. As Silva started work, however, he began to see that the firm's problems were cultural and not merely financial in nature. He believed that the paternalism of the past had led to many inefficiencies and a harboring of "dead wood" in the company. He was convinced the continuation of this culture would lead to the demise of the company. He commented: "I like to define culture as the personality of the company, and so I think there are two ways to change that personality. The first is by long-term change, where you gradually work at some of the problem areas in the culture. The second is trauma, where you massively address the company problems" (McKinnon, 1983a, p. 16).

After six months on the job Silva believed that massive cultural change was the answer to the company's woes. Wally Bennett resigned, and the company began laying off or firing many long-term employees. Silva cut more than 40 percent of the work force—and in so doing helped the company become profitable again. Senator Bennett strongly supported Silva's decisions, much to the chagrin of many family members. Company old-timers were outraged. One wrote in a letter to the editor of a local paper: "I'm glad 83-year-old Wallace Bennett and

30-year-old Mike Silva can now sleep well at night. I can appreciate all businesses have to be reassessed and changed, but at the expense of some employees who have worked 30–40 years and are 1–5 years away from retirement? Ruthless only describes the method used to terminate dedicated employees. Selfish is the more appropriate term for those who succeeded in doing a job that requires no business talent" (McKinnon, 1983b, p. 14).

Despite such criticism, Silva commented: "This is the ugly part of this whole change effort. But to keep unproductive managers would send the wrong message to everyone else in the company. The old company fostered a system that created these managers and attitudes. The managers we had couldn't quite do it, couldn't quite pull it together in our new system. It was a hard thing to do; there were letters to the editors and everything. But I'm ruthless with executives. These guys are a commodity" (McKinnon, 1983b, p. 4).

Silva's famous "Iron Curtain" and the "closed door" policy insulated him against the attacks of those who would undermine the new regime. With the company profitable again, much of the criticism subsided. He rewarded his top company officers with large bonuses and all-expense-paid vacations for their families to anywhere in the world. With Senator Bennett's support and encouragement, Michael Silva transformed Bennett Enterprises into his version of an "excellent company."

Mr. and Mrs. Jones, Inc. Mr. and Mrs. Jones, Inc. (a fictional name) was founded by Mrs. Jones, with her husband's financial backing, in the mid-1970s (Brown, 1985b). The company sells a variety of baked goods. Starting with only one store, Mr. and Mrs. Jones have built a worldwide network of stores with sales of over $30 million in only a few years. Mr. and Mrs. Jones started their enterprise with a well-articulated philosophy that they believed their employees should follow. The major features of this philosophy include:

1. The company is "value driven." This means that our values, not profits, are the driving force behind the company.
2. People are important. The company cares about both its customers and its employees.

3. We are a family; we work as a team.
4. Quality will not be compromised.
5. Service to the customer will be given with enthusiasm.

With the tremendous growth of the company in the early 1980s, the Joneses decided to bring in professional management to run the day-to-day affairs of the firm. The business had grown too large to operate by themselves. However, the professionals they hired were skeptical of the Jones philosophy and all that it entailed. Mrs. Jones believes with a passion that by following these values the individual employee and the company will succeed. Some of the professional managers thought otherwise. Employees soon began to see a discrepancy between the Jones' philosophy and the behavior of the new managers. The new management stressed profit, not values. They knew little about product quality and felt that Mrs. Jones' passion for enthusiastic service was a bit "corny." The professional managers recommended that store managers be responsible for more than one store, and soon the store managers were less aware of the local clientele and the day-to-day activities of an individual store. Reams of memos directing store managers to change their operations went out from the corporate offices. Mr. and Mrs. Jones initially gave the new managers a rather free hand in implementing their ideas since, as Mr. Jones put it: "They seemed to know what they were doing and we wanted some new ideas."

The consequences of the professional managers' recommendations were disastrous. Employee morale suffered. There were mass resignations in some stores. Quality and customer service deteriorated. Profitability declined. At this point Mr. and Mrs. Jones intervened to stop the professional managers from, as Mr. Jones put it, "bringing the company to its knees." The professional managers were told that they could no longer send any memos to the stores without the prior approval of Mr. or Mrs. Jones. From that point on, the company would be run the family's way—or not at all. Some of the professionals stayed but with smaller roles and less responsibility. One Jones employee described the professional managers that remain at the company: "Professional managers are like chameleons. You flop them down and they turn yellow on this thing, then turn red on another. They go whichever way the wind blows. And the wind here is only blowing one direction . . . Mr. and Mrs. Jones' way'' (Brown, 1985b, p. 10).

Mr and Mrs. Jones believe that they are now well on their way to changing the company culture and ridding it of the ideas brought by their professional managers. Although the move to professional management seemed to be a good idea at the time, in retrospect the Joneses believe they would have done things quite differently if they had been aware of some of the consequences.

The Goldschmidt Corporation. The Goldschmidt Corporation (fictional name) was founded by Bernard Goldschmidt in the early 1920s. He started with one small grocery store, which eventually expanded to a large grocery and department store chain with sales over $1 billion. Mr. Goldschmidt ran the business as an autocrat, allowing only a few trusted professional managers into his inner circle. Bernard had four daughters—no sons— and this was a disappointment for him since he felt that none of his daughters had the ability to manage the business. Over time his sons-in-law came into the business but none of them met his expectations either. Bernard could not bear to think about retirement or plan for succession. Phillip Henderson, his trusted aide, tried to counsel Bernard to think about planning for succession but stopped after realizing how painful this was for him. Without naming a successor, Bernard died in the late 1970s. Chaos reigned until Phillip Henderson agreed to become interim president for five years. During this period Henderson experienced a multitude of conflicts and problems, particularly from Bernard's oldest daughter, who was vying with other family members for the top position. In this climate Henderson complained: "They're always thinking about the needs of the family— never about the business. We need to be concerned about the business as a economic unit.''

Henderson felt that the squabbles within the family (who also owned the business) and their disagreements with professional managers were jeopardizing the profitability of the business and the hundreds of jobs in the company. He himself was about to retire, and he found family members wanting in managerial talent, so he urged that another professional manager be brought in. An outside professional was hired, but this further exacerbated the differences between the family and professional management. Henderson's power had been based on his prior relationship with Bernard Goldschmidt and his knowledge of the family and the business. His successor, with none of these assets, was forced to resign within a year and a half. In this organization the presidency has become a revolving door.

With the family incapable of managing the business, the professional managers are often put in an impossible situation: they must yield to the whims of family members while attempting to run the business. Under this set of rules the company is facing a crisis of leadership for many years to come.

The Role of Professional Management

These three examples highlight a number of different roles the professional manager may play in the process of culture change. In Bennett Enterprises the professional manager was the instrument of culture change. The mandate Michael Silva received from Senator Wallace Bennett was to "clean house" and create a more "efficient" system based on a new set of assumptions.

In the case of Mr. and Mrs. Jones, the mandate given to the professional managers was not to change the culture but to implement the values and carry out the values and beliefs of the family. This became troublesome when the family and professional managers found their values at odds. Those professionals who survive at Mr. and Mrs. Jones, Inc. must follow the company philosophy to the letter or they are forced to leave.

The professional managers in the Goldschmidt Corporation found themselves trying to save the firm from some of the more destructive influences of the family. They became primarily "family mediators" acting as a buffer between firm and family. In the absence of ownership power, however, the professionals often found themselves fighting a losing battle. The family was able to fire the professionals if they did not live up to their standards. Such practices can easily lead to a "revolving door syndrome," where the firm experiences frequent leadership changes and very weak leaders.

Thus we see that role of professional managers may differ greatly from company to company, depending on the cultures of the family, the business, and the governing board.

Making the Decision

Taking a company public or bringing in professional management involves major transitions for the firm; these decisions are not to be made lightly. In Chapter Eight, we will discuss in detail the process of making the profound transitions that these changes bring. But first, founders should make every effort to look at the issue fully. To help in this process, we present some questions founders should confront.

Should the Firm Go Public?

1. Will I be able to satisfy the short-term needs of outside shareholders and still maintain a focus on the long-term viability of the business?
2. Can I handle the stock market pressures for constant increases in sales and earnings?
3. Will I be able to accept outside review of my decisions and mistakes?
4. Will I be able to distribute stock to both family and non-family members in a way that will avoid serious conflicts?
5. Why do I want to go public in the first place? What are my motives?
6. What is the potential for undesirable consequences that might result from going public?

If, after answering these questions, the family feels that going public is in their best interest, plans should be made to anticipate and manage some of the major problems. The family must develop a way to avoid the trap of focusing only on short-run results and attempt to develop reward and promotion criteria that will eliminate the undesirable effects of competition.

Should Professional Management Be Brought In?

1. Is it necessary to hire outside professional management? Do I currently lack the needed skills or abilities?
2. Will professional management change the culture in positive or negative ways? What are the tradeoffs?
3. How will the family relate to professional management? What impact will professional management have on the careers of family members?
4. What are my motives for bringing in professional management? What role will they play?
5. What criteria should I use in choosing professional managers?

After answering these questions, the family should be able to list the pros and cons of bringing in professional management and take steps to manage some of the problems that we have discussed.

There are a few strategies that can help to make a smooth transition when professional managers are brought in. First, if the family wishes to retain many of the values and beliefs held by the employees, they should avoid bringing in outside managers during crisis periods if at all possible. Managers entering during a crisis tend to make sweeping changes that dramatically change the nature of the business. Second, taking time to socialize new managers so they will be able to understand the nature of the firm's culture is critical to helping them function effectively. Not only must they know the product and the customers, but they must also understand what things the family values. If Mr. and Mrs. Jones had done this, many of the problems they encountered could have been avoided. Finally, because professional managers are likely to bring with them perspectives, values, and assumptions that are at odds with those of the family and local work force, skills in managing conflict are essential. What the family generally wants to do is get the best of both worlds—the family's commitment to a particular kind of business, and the new ideas brought by professional management. To create this kind of synergy often requires the use of the conflict management interventions discussed in Chapter Five.

Part Three

Managing Family Firms
Successfully and
Ensuring Continuity

Up to this point we have described the evolution of family firms, their cultural patterns, and their problems. In Part Three, we will describe what can be done to manage the family firm successfully over its life cycle to ensure continuity. As we have discovered, the problems are great and highly complex. Preparing for and managing transitions is not easy.

Chapter Seven is probably the most important in the entire book; it presents the conditions in the business, the family, and the board of directors that are needed for successful transitions to take place. Founders must be willing to relinquish power and prepare the next generation for leadership responsibilities. The family members must be able to trust one another and work out their disagreements peacefully. The board of directors must provide expertise to help the family through the problems surrounding succession. If these things can be done, the probability of a successful transition is greatly enhanced.

Managing change in the family firm is the topic of Chapter Eight. It describes how to gather data about the cultures of family firms, how to identify key problems, and how to select, implement, and evaluate different change strategies. Four different types of problems—individual, interpersonal, intergroup, and organizational—are described, along with the change strategies associated with each type.

The final chapter presents twelve signs of a healthy firm. If a family firm fails to develop these twelve attributes, the business and family are likely to fail. This chapter describes a common fault of leaders of family firms: they are often too "solution oriented" and must learn to "manage the process" rather than merely search for a solution. Finally, the chapter describes one critical key to success in a family firm: enlightened leadership.

Seven

Handling Key Transitions Effectively

One of the major purposes of studying family businesses histor-
ically was to gain a better understanding of those conditions and
dynamics that accompany successful leadership transitions between generations. By examining the conditions in each of the
three components—the business, the governing board, and the
family—before, during, and after a transition, we were able to
see why some family businesses had managed change well and
why others were obvious failures. We looked at the general
economic health of the business, changes in ownership and management patterns, and cultural changes in each firm. Although
data for a complete analysis were lacking in some cases, there
appeared to be remarkable consistency in the attributes of successful firms.

In this chapter we will outline the conditions that lead
to success—and failure—in managing transitions between generations and describe the kinds of cultural configurations that
help or hinder a family firm during a transition.

What Is a "Successful" Transition?

As we examined our panel of family businesses during
various transition periods, it became evident that differentiating
the "successful" from the "unsuccessful" would not be easy.
Some firms, for instance, made a transition that was successful
from the standpoint of the business, but family relationships were
virtually destroyed. Other firms maintained harmony within the
family at the expense of the business. Because most consider

both firm and family important, we decided that a successful transition would be one where *both* business and family were relatively effective after the transition had taken place.

With this in mind, several criteria were used to determine effectiveness. For the business:

1. Profitability.
2. Ability to adapt to new conditions.
3. Innovation (development of new products or markets).
4. Growth (in terms of sales and number of employees).
5. Job satisfaction (represented by strikes or turnover).

These criteria are clearly not exhaustive, but they do give us a general picture of how the business fared after the transition.

Criteria for determining family effectiveness included:

1. The ability of the family to meet a member's basic needs and wants.
2. Ability to solve problems and meet threats facing the family.
3. Existence of satisfactory family relationships.

With these criteria, we attempted to discover whether the family remained intact, with the ability to solve problems and achieve some sense of satisfaction from family members.

Using these criteria (or any criteria, for that matter) to judge business and family effectiveness has its shortcomings. What is effective for one family or organization may not be effective for another. Measuring and evaluating these criteria are also problematic. Despite these difficulties, however, as we began to study the transitions of the family businesses in our panel and analyze their impact on the business and the family, these criteria seemed to provide a reasonable measuring stick. In a few cases, it was difficult, if not impossible, to ascertain effectiveness because we either lacked data or saw mixed signals. In most cases, however, the signals were clear. Some firms failed or declined dramatically. Others lost key people or lost their sense of purpose and direction. Some families lost much of their wealth or were torn with dissension and hostility. Other families became paralyzed when it came to problem solving. In such firms determining effectiveness was relatively easy.

Thirty of the more than forty firms in our panel had experienced major leadership and organizational transitions. Of those thirty, we concluded that twelve were successful and eighteen unsuccessful. The rest either had not gone through a major transition or were lacking sufficient data to assess family or organizational effectiveness.

Conditions Favoring Successful Transitions

In those firms that had made successful transitions, we found eleven common factors in the business, the family, and the governing board. Not all were present in all cases, but it appeared that the likelihood of success increased if all eleven conditions held.

Conditions in the Business

The key factors for a successful business transition were the overall "health" of the organization at the time the transition took place and the degree to which the family had prepared for a change in leadership.

The "Health" of the Business. Timing appears to play a crucial role in making a transition successful. Those firms that managed transitions well had developed a well-conceived set of products, clear markets, and efficient technologies to produce and distribute their products. They had created a market niche or a distinctive competence for which they were known, such as IBM's reputation for service or Procter & Gamble's emphasis on marketing. The founders and their families had the skills to carry out their business strategies. With the business solidly grounded, the family could make the transition without a great deal of tension and uncertainty.

Many of the unsuccessful families, however, delayed making transitions during good times; they seemed guided by the philosophy "If it ain't broke, don't fix it." Unfortunately, the firm inevitably came upon hard times, and family members or other investors applied tremendous pressure for a change. When resources are perceived to be shrinking, family members and others scramble to protect their investments and power. In a climate of fear and uncertainty, the family often makes knee-jerk responses, fails to consider the long-term implications of its actions, and feels forced to make changes. Firms such as Genesco, Disney, National Cash Register, and International Harvester did not fare well during their transition periods because of the many organizational problems that precipitated the changes.

Although it is quite apparent that a business would be better off making a transition during a halcyon period rather than a turbulent one, many unsuccessful families wait until the crisis occurs before taking any action. Of course, such crises are often difficult to predict, but the clear implication for a family business is: If you have a choice and can forecast the future with reasonable accuracy, make the transition when things are going well. If the business is doing well now and a transition appears imminent (because of the founder's age or health, for instance), begin the transition process as soon as possible.

Founder's Involvement Declines. As mentioned in Chapter Four, founders and other leaders of family business often have a strong desire for power and control. Much of the meaning in their lives is derived from creating an organization and fulfilling their needs through it. The tendency to hold on to "their baby" is all too common. Given this orientation, founders and other leaders strongly resist any attempt to change their status. Retirement is a death sentence. One founder of a Latin American conglomerate described his feelings about succession this way: "The basic dilemma is that succession planning by a founder is really . . . digging your own grave. It's preparing for your own death and it's very difficult to make contact with the concept of death emotionally. . . . It is a kind of *seppuku*—the *harakiri* that Japanese commit. [It's like] putting a dagger to your belly . . . and having someone behind you cut off your head. . . . That analogy sounds dramatic, but emotionally it's close to it. You're ripping yourself apart—your power, your significance, your leadership, your father role, your chief executive role, and your founder role" (Beckhard and Dyer, 1983b, pp. 60, 61).

In the firms that had difficulty, the founders attempted to run all aspects of the business until they died, were incapacitated, or were forced to retire. One nonfamily executive in our panel revealed that he had tried time and time again to get the founder of the company to plan for succession. Discussing succession was too painful for the founder and the executive eventually gave up. When the founder died there was great turmoil in the family and the business because no family member was prepared to manage the business. Both the family and the firm have had serious problems since the founder's death, with no solution in sight.

One of the more bizarre cases of a founder attempting to hold on to his business involves the Wilson Stove Company (fictional name). Thomas Wilson bought what was to become the Wilson Stove Company after fifteen years as a loyal employee. The company sold coal-burning stoves that were superior in design to most competitors' products. To help manage the business, Thomas brought in his brother Alvin. The brothers managed the business quite profitably for many years until Thomas wanted to retire. As Alvin began to take over operations from Thomas, he expanded the product line to include fiberglass boats. This proved to be a major mistake, and the firm suffered serious losses. Realizing that the company he helped to build might be lost, Thomas rejoined the business and eventually sold the fiberglass boat division.

Thomas Wilson ostensibly still wanted to retire. However, he felt that Alvin could not be trusted to run the company so he began to look for outside buyers. He finally sold the firm to a group of businessmen in a neighboring state, but they quickly proved to be incompetent managers. Thomas, still interested in the business, was aware of these problems and eventually decided to buy back the business. Five more times in a period of less than five years, Thomas sold the business only to buy it back again because the new owners were either incompetent or were not running the business the way he felt it should be run. In 1984 Thomas Wilson was still looking for a buyer.

We might be tempted to call this an unusual run of bad luck for Thomas Wilson. But in a deeper sense, this case illustrates the problems that occur when a founder is unable to move away from his business and let others manage it. At the first sign of trouble, Wilson would step in immediately to buy back the business. He paid little attention to training new owners. He *said* he wanted to retire, but all his actions indicate otherwise. He was so attached emotionally to the firm that he could not bear to see it in what he believed were incompetent hands. Of course, we may never know Wilson's true motives, but it is possible that he sold the firm to individuals that he believed would fail. Thus he would never really have to retire and could always be in a position to "save" his company.

In successful transitions, the founders or family leaders are generally aware of the motives behind their plans to move away from active operations in the firm. Without such self-insight and the ability to accept the fact that eventually a new generation of managers will manage their organizations, the founders are likely to experience a great deal of personal pain. And such negative personal experiences are likely to affect both the family and the business. In some cases where founders did make preparations to move away from the business, it took a serious illness or some other dramatic event to motivate them to deal with the issue of succession. Developing interests outside the business also helps to make the transition easier. One founder currently planning for succession intends to spend more time with his family and in civic affairs and local clubs. Without some alternative activities that are stimulating to the "old" leaders, they will be unwilling to make way for the next generation.

Training and Socializing Successors. Having the founder plan to disengage from the business is necessary, but by itself it is not sufficient to ensure a successful transition. The other ingredient is a competent replacement; otherwise the family firm can be in serious trouble. One study, for example, attributed 45 percent of all business failures to incompetent new management (McGivern, 1978).

Family members often come in contact with the business at an early age. They may visit their father or mother at work, and as they get older may work at the business on weekends or during the summer. Conversations at the dinner table frequently deal with business topics. In many family businesses we studied, the children of the founder were introduced into the business almost from birth. In some, entering the business was equated with a "divine calling," and tremendous pressure was exerted on family members to rise to a leadership position in the firm. Unfortunately, this "dinner-table training" does not ensure competent management in the next generation. There are, however, a number of training strategies that have proven quite valuable.

In firms such as Du Pont and Levi Strauss, younger family members are often encouraged to attend one of the top universities such as MIT, Stanford, or Harvard. Some families believe that a degree from one of these schools is a sign of intelligence and indicates that the family member is a leader. The college or technical degree is the first hurdle that potential successors must overcome.

Once they enter the business, family members may experience a variety of career paths. Some of the more successful family businesses put potential successors through a program in which they "work their way up" the organization and prove themselves. This was the approach used by the Neiman-Marcus family. Stanley Marcus, son of the founder, describes the process used to get his son Dick ready to assume major responsibilities (Marcus, 1974, p. 268):

> [Dick] has passed through various positions in the store, from buying to merchandising to store management with success at all stages. Having lived through the problems of a family dominated business, I must admit I leaned over backwards to avoid any charge of nepotism so far as Dick was concerned and no doubt I have expected higher standards of performance from him than I have from others. When my brother Edward decided to retire from the store to devote his full time to his extensive real estate interests, I had no idea who his replacement might be. I was not sure that Dick was ready or that he possessed the combination of qualities neces-

sary to fill the job. We interviewed candidates from all over the country, and when we had talked to the last one, one of my associates said, "You've got the best-qualified person in the entire country right here in the store. You're being unduly tough on him just because he happens to be your own son." I made a reappraisal of Dick, concluding that my associate was right, and recommended that Dick be named president. I moved to the position of chairman of the board and chief executive officer, thus enabling me to give Dick on-the-job training in the problems and techniques of administering the affairs of an expanding business. He has responded to his new responsibilities even better than I might have hoped, earning the respect and cooperation of the entire organization. By the time of my retirement, he will be well qualified to carry on the objectives of Neiman-Marcus in the manner enunciated by his grandfather.

By giving his son a variety of experiences and tasks, Stanley Marcus was able to provide the necessary training. He also encouraged him to build the kind of relationships with nonfamily members that would help him run the business in the future.

Stanley Marcus used another training tactic frequently found in family firms—a "mentor." The mentor (who may or may not be a family member) is the personal counselor, confidant, and instructor for the future successor. Mentors are usually found in important positions within the firm. They use their knowledge of the culture of the business, the governing board, and the family to teach the neophyte all the subtle nuances associated with being a manager in the family-dominated enterprise.

Another strategy for training family members is to let them have experience outside the business first. At the same time they are gaining valuable experience, they are also assessing their interest in joining the family business. In some families the family member is given relevant experience by leading a subsidiary or a division under the auspices of the family. In either case, the goal is to allow the future leaders to gain additional experience.

In a few of the successful family businesses we studied, no family member was available as a successor, for various reasons. One firm that dealt with this problem successfully was the F. Steel Company described by Hollander (1984). The nonfamily member who became the president was able to succeed because of his longstanding relationship with the family. The family trusted him, he was seen as competent, and he came from the same ethnic background as the family. Thus the new leader was aware of the culture of the family and the firm and could act consistently with the family's basic values and assumptions.

Another family firm, Fiat, Italy's largest private industrial group, was not as fortunate. In 1976, the Agnelli family hired an outsider, Carlo de Benedetti, to become managing director. He lasted only 100 days. Apparently, de Benedetti was not well versed in the culture of a company that the family head, Giovanni Agnelli, describes as "always really run by the same people. This means we have enormous trust in each other and know what we can do" ("Fiat Chairman Giovanni Agnelli . . . ," p. 36). Agnelli saw de Benedetti's failure to gain the trust of this group as a function of his attempts to "be [the] boss in our home." De Benedetti replied, "If you are king like Mr. Agnelli, you are for the monarchy. If you're not, you're a republican. I am a republican and he is a king" (p. 36). Such differences of opinion led quickly to de Benedetti's ouster.

If a nonfamily member or an "outsider" assumes the leadership role in a family business, it is important that they be made aware of the key facets of the culture of both firm and family. Without such knowledge, nonfamily executives are likely to make some serious errors that damage their credibility. If this occurs, managing any transition can prove hazardous.

Interdependent Relationships with Successors. The fourth factor that differentiates successful from unsuccessful firms concerns the relationship between founder and successor. As described in Chapters Two and Four, relationships in family businesses can be classified as interdependent, counterdependent, or dependent.

Families that have either a counterdependent or dependent relationship between generations often have great difficulty. The founders either find themselves in the position of turning

over the business to someone they distrust or have strong disagreements with, or they find that their replacement lacks the
necessary leadership skills to provide direction. When such relationships are present, a rocky transition is a natural consequence.

Interdependent relationships tend to create two conditions
that favor a successful transition. First, the founders and their
organizations benefit because the successors bring with them
a set of attributes or skills that are needed for the firm's future
development. The newcomers make a major contribution. Sec-
ondly, the future leaders feel a need to learn from the current
leadership. Thus the leaders of the business are able to inculcate
some of their basic beliefs upon the next generation of leaders.
In this way both generations benefit from the relationship, and
such relationships pave the way for a smooth transition.

Willard Marriott and his son Bill, Jr., were apparently
able to create such a relationship. Willard Marriott took his
knowledge of the restaurant industry and his ability to provide
quality service and built a small root-beer stand into a multimillion-dollar corporation in a relatively short time. The elder
Marriott was very conservative, avoiding debt whenever possible. This philosophy tended to slow the firm's growth. Bill, Jr.,
however, was well trained in finance and understood the benefits
of using debt to finance various projects—particularly the Marriott Hotels. Although Willard Marriott initially resisted his son's
efforts to expand using debt, he eventually relented; the company continued to prosper, in fact grew more rapidly than ever.
Furthermore, Bill, Jr., learned much of his philosophy of business from his father, and it served him well as he planned for
expansion. In this kind of relationship both men benefited. This
made the transition from father to son a smooth one and helped
to turn the company into a billion-dollar business.

As we outlined in Chapter Four, creating an interdependent relationship requires that leaders and their successors do
certain things. The leaders must be willing to spend the time
to teach and train their successors—without resenting the fact
that they will eventually be turning over the reins of power. They
must be willing to delegate appropriate and significant responsibility to the next generation to allow them to gain experience

and to demonstrate to themselves and others that they are competent. The successors, for their part, must learn patience, must be willing to listen and learn from the leaders. They must also think about the kind of skills and abilities that the company will need in the future, so they can plan their education and training. Open communication is crucial to build trust and create a climate where both parties can work closely together. These kinds of relationships do not just happen; they are a product of a great deal of time and effort.

Conditions in the Family

As we studied the family units of those family businesses that were able to make smooth transitions, we found that the key factors were the families' views on equity, planning, conflict resolution, goals, and interpersonal relationships. Sometimes there were other factors as well, but these conditions were the most common.

Consistent Views of Equity. The family's view of what is "fair" and "equitable" is often the one factor underpinning many of the problems experienced during a transition period. If family members feel that they are not receiving their fair share, they often attempt to undermine the efforts of others in order to achieve a more equitable distribution of company stock, power, or assets. Decision making is often slowed down dramatically. Generally matters are resolved in one of two ways: the "poorer" family members are bought out, or the disagreements are settled in a courtroom.

When we speak of "consistent" views of equity, we do not mean that all family members feel they receive *equal* treatment but that any differences in stock or assets are a function of some criteria—experience, expertise, commitment—that family members recognize as valid. For example, if one family member is compensated more because she spends more time working in the business, that is generally seen as equitable. Determining what criteria are relevant, how to measure them, and how to resolve disagreements are often serious problems, but somehow the successful family firm manages to make those determinations.

Clarifying expectations and role negotiation can also be used to manage the equity problem. Even family members who experience some inequities in the short run tend to be committed to resolving differences if they believe that—through a process of clarifying expectations—many of the disparities will be alleviated in the long run.

Planning for Contingencies. The psychological and emotional issues surrounding succession and change that confront founders often prevent them from planning for contingencies. Estate planning is put off; even if accomplished, it may not be revealed to other family members. One study of small-business owners indicated that over 95 percent had not had detailed discussions with their spouses concerning the disposition of their estates if they were to die (Lewis, 1978). Another study conducted some years ago noted that those businesses that had developed a succession plan and had communicated the details were more able to remain profitable after succession than those businesses that failed to plan (Trow, 1961).

Death is not the only contingency that requires attention. What happens if the founder is incapacitated by a serious illness? What happens if those designated to be successors die or experience other problems that disqualify them? Many families seem to believe "That could never happen to us!" Unfortunately, based on the experiences of the firms we studied, the unexpected *does* happen all too often, and the family is forced to make some undesirable choices. For those who have not planned for it, estate taxes often prove to be an overwhelming burden. Sometimes the only answer is to sell the business to pay the tax. In the case of the Brown Corporation, the family would have been forced to sell the business if John Brown, Sr., had not recovered from his bout with pancreatitis. Families must think through the potential emergencies that could arise and develop contingency plans to deal with them.

Mechanisms to Manage Conflict. Another attribute of families that handle change well is their ability to manage conflict. As mentioned in Chapter Five, family firms can create asset management boards consisting of family members and nonfamily executives to manage disputes. Sometimes the founder's spouse or a trusted executive may act as a mediator; their skill in managing conflict can determine the outcome of a transition. Other conflict management mechanisms are also used in successful family firms.

Unfortunately, the cultural patterns created by most powerful, charismatic leaders do not lend themselves well to resolving conflict. Founders tend to control, manage, and quell dissent, permitting little input from others in the decision-making process. Without the founder, the second generation is often left with no history of decision making and no ability to manage conflict. Some families, such as the Du Ponts and the Boss family at A. T. Cross, had such deep disagreements that warring factions would not even talk to one another. They had no mechanisms available within their family or organization to mediate the conflicts, so they resorted to the courts. Once the legal system becomes the mediator, the effect on family relationships is devastating, for it is an admission that the family has failed.

Superordinate Goals. One of the most powerful forces that can help families make a transition is having superordinate goals that the entire family can agree on and strive to achieve. The tendency in family firms is to do the opposite: to fight for individual self-interest rather than explore what might be in the best interest of all parties.

Some of the families we studied had a desire to carry on the legacy of the founder, and family members subordinated their own needs to carry out this mandate. In others, the goal was to preserve the family wealth or to avoid damaging conflicts that could tear the family apart. The goal of maintaining family control of the business often created the impetus for cooperation. In a few cases, the family's goal was to maximize wealth in the short run, and so selling the business for the right price was the superordinate goal. Without a set of goals and objectives that bind the family together, division and strife are often the result.

High Levels of Trust. The level of trust that exists among family members and nonfamily employees is one of the most important factors contributing to a successful transition. Transitions necessarily involve some anxiety and uncertainty. Those families that are able to trust and rely on others can risk being open and can make difficult decisions in a supportive climate. Without relatively honest and informed communication, the family is unlikely to make the best decisions during transition periods.

Lack of trust can be devastating. In some cases, such as Du Pont and A. T. Cross Company, a few family members created a climate of distrust by attempting to gain control of their companies via a secret purchase of stock. When the other family members found out, the battle lines were drawn and prolonged conflicts ensued. Once trust is destroyed, regaining it is extraordinarily difficult.

Conditions of Governing Boards

The boards of directors also played a role in the success of managing transitions. Two of the most prominent roles concern the distribution of power in the firm and using board members' expertise to solve problems.

Power Clarity. One of the more serious problems that plague a family business during a transition concerns the use and distribution of power. During the founder's tenure, the locus of power is generally quite clear, but as the family prepares to make a transition, the distribution of power may change greatly.

Those family firms that make smooth transitions tend to prepare for the transfer of power and determine who will ultimately be in control, before the transition begins. When there is uncertainty, conflicts inevitably arise. Consider the case of Du Pont in the mid-1800s. During this period, General Henry Du Pont was the undisputed leader of the business. Henry failed to designate any successor, and when he died each of his two sons, Henry, Jr., and William, felt that he should be the next president. After protracted debates among board and family members, it became apparent that neither brother had sufficient support to defeat the other. Stalemated, the family looked for an acceptable alternative and eventually chose Eugene Du Pont to succeed Henry. Such a succession process reduced Eugene to a caretaker, and the schism between Henry, Jr., and William was never resolved. In fact, this conflict created even greater divisions in the family, which made future transitions even more difficult to manage.

In other cases, too, the ambiguity surrounding the power relationships during a transition can generate debilitating conflicts. The role of the board of directors in the successful family firm is to clarify power relationships before, during, and after the transition and to minimize the deleterious consequences of power struggles.

Board Expertise. The experience and expertise of board members can also be decisive in making a successful transition. This expertise can range from giving financial advice, to making the right connections on the outside, to mediating conflicts. As we saw earlier, the Brown Corporation's family banker, who served on the board, was instrumental in healing a major rift between John Brown, Jr., and his father.

Often family firms are hesitant to place outside directors on the board. But if carefully selected, outside board members can be extremely valuable assets to the family firm in transition.

Relationship Among the Conditions for Successful Transitions

The eleven conditions outlined above describe the attributes of those firms that were able to make a successful transition. Although each focuses on a different issue, they are clearly not independent. Founders who plan to move away from active involvement in the business generally develop a training program for their successors. Families with high trust are more likely to have superordinate goals and interdependent relationships. Certain cultural patterns—particularly the participative patterns in the firm and collaborative patterns in the family— are more likely to produce these conditions. Thus in evaluating the likelihood that any given organization will make a successful transition, it is important not only to see how many of these conditions are present, but also to put them into an overall context, a *gestalt*, if you will, to understand how the cultural configuration and these conditions relate to one another.

High-Risk Cultural Configurations. As we compared successful and unsuccessful firms, we found that some cultural configurations had a higher incidence of failure. The typical configuration of firms that had difficulty was (1) a paternalistic
business, (2) a conflicted or patriarchal family, and (3) a paper
or rubber-stamp board. Firms with these cultural patterns seemed
unable to foster many of the conditions of success. In a paternalistic organization, the family leader is unlikely to plan for
transitions; whereas the power is clear during the leader's tenure,
often an ambiguous power vacuum is left when the transition
takes place. Such leaders generally fail to plan for contingencies and prepare the next generation to assume leadership roles.
Family members are either so dependent on the leader or so
embroiled in conflict that decision making is often poor and trust
between family members suffers. Without any review or input
from competent board members, the family is unable to recognize their weaknesses or mediate their differences. They rush
headlong toward disaster, oblivious to the consequences of their
actions.

Configurations of Success. On the other hand, the successful
family firm typically had (1) a laissez-faire or participative business culture, (2) a collaborative family culture, and (3) an advisory board. This configuration created a family firm that fostered trust, collaboration, and teamwork in the business. The
company was future oriented and had planned for succession
and unexpected contingencies. The owning family had developed
mechanisms to handle conflict, trusted one another, and had
shared goals and values. They had also been able to find competent advisers to help them through the transition.

Families that are successful are generally aware of the problems that confront them. They are able to look objectively at
the family and firm and plan to meet the essential needs of both
as best they can. They are aware of the tradeoffs that must be
made when making decisions about the future of the family and
the business and have a sense of balancing priorities between
the two systems. When nothing is important except business
success, family relations suffer. On the other hand, when family
concerns dominate totally, the business loses. One family went
so far as to have family members trade the job of company presi-

dent every month or so to avoid hurting anyone's feelings. Such a "solution," while avoiding some family conflicts, is certainly not likely to create a strong business with coherent leadership. When thinking about managing transitions, the family must perform a balancing act, meeting the needs of the family *and* the business.

A summary of the conditions favoring successful transitions in the family firm follows.

Business Conditions

1. The transition occurred when the organization was relatively "healthy."
2. The founder moved gradually away from active involvement in the firm's operations.
3. There was a well-developed training and socialization program for the successor.
4. There was an interdependent relationship between the founders and their successors.

Family Conditions

1. The family shared common views concerning equity.
2. The family had planned for emergencies and other contingencies.
3. The family had developed mechanisms to resolve conflict.
4. The family shared superordinate goals.
5. High trust existed among family members.

Board Conditions

1. Power relationships were clear—little ambiguity.
2. The board had the necessary expertise to manage problems of both the firm and family.

Eight

Determining Culturally Based Problems and Initiating Change

Managing change in a family firm offers a number of challenges not found in other kinds of organizations. Business problems *and* family issues must be handled. In Chapter Three, we described what happens when family firms are not prepared to manage change and crisis: changes in leadership, conflict, and power struggles in the business are typical. The continuity of family values and relationships is often jeopardized. To avoid some of the unpleasant side effects of crisis and change, leaders of family business can take steps to manage the change process incrementally rather than let the change process manage them (Quinn, 1980). By modifying the firm's artifacts, perspectives, values—and at times even basic assumptions—the business and the family can evolve into "healthier" conditions and avoid crisis and revolution.

It is possible to think of the process for managing change in five steps. Although the steps seem rather simple, managers of family firms are often unaware of this process or do not know how to carry it out.

Step 1. Assess Cultural Patterns

The first step involves gathering data about the cultural patterns in the family firm—the business, the family, and the governing board. "Mapping" the three cultures can be done in a number of ways.

138

Gathering Data About the Business. Gathering data about a family firm's artifacts, perspectives, values, and assumptions takes time and effort. Three major sources of the business culture—the founder's philosophy, the problems of basic survival, and the problems individuals face as they enter the family business—are useful starting points.

Because founders are a key source of information about the organization's culture, it is generally useful to ask:

1. Why was the organization founded? What was the founder trying to achieve?
2. What was the founder's management "philosophy"? Was it formalized? How did the founder attempt to implement the philosophy?
3. What specific artifacts, perspectives, values, and assumptions are associated with the founder?

The business' response to the problems of survival are often the key to understanding basic values. To gather such data one might ask:

1. What major crises has the organization confronted? How did the organization deal with these crises?
2. What major changes have occurred in the organization's
   a. Strategy
   b. Structure
   c. Technology
   d. Size
   e. Leadership
   How and why were these changes made? How did the changes affect the organization?
3. How does the organization reward and control its members?
4. How are decisions made?
5. What is the nature of relationships between employees?

To determine how individuals function in the business, one might learn:

1.   What are the organization's socialization practices?
2.   What does an employee need to know or do to become an accepted member of the organization?
3.   Which employees have been successful and which have failed? Why?
4.   How does one gain power and influence?
5.   How do employees get noticed and get their ideas adopted?
6.   Who are the "heroes" and who are the "villains"? Why?

Gathering Data About the Family. The process of asking the questions above, on the culture of the business, will also reveal much about the culture of the governing boards and family as well. However, to learn more about the culture of the family, we must look further:

1.   What are the relationships between the founder and the children? Between the founder and his or her spouse?
2.   What do family members see as the purpose of the business?
3.   What criteria are used to determine whether or not a family member goes into the business? What are the promotion criteria?
4.   Has the founder or family planned for succession? What estate planning has been done?
5.   What major problems has the family had to overcome? What problems does it now face?
6.   How does the family handle disagreements? How are decisions made?

Gathering Data About the Board. To understand the cultural patterns of the governing board, one should ask:

1.   What is the role of the board of directors or other governing boards?
2.   What criteria are used for selecting board members?
3.   What major problems or issues has the board handled and how did it solve them? What are the current issues it faces?
4.   Who wields the most influence on the board? Why?

5. How are board decisions made (participative or authoritarian)?

These are certainly not all the questions that could be explored when studying a family firm. If one delves deeper into
the dynamics of any given firm, new questions and hypotheses
inevitably arise. Still, these questions are a useful starting point.

To begin to answer these questions, we must gather as
much data as we can. Available sources include:

1. *Key Family Members and Employees.* Family members, board
members, key executives, and long-term employees who are
knowledgeable about the business and the family are the most
valuable sources of information. Small-group discussions and interviews are useful vehicles to gather data from these individuals.

2. *Outside Informants.* Data can be gathered from customers, suppliers, and consultants who have worked with the firm.
Outside sources often present different points of view from ''insiders,'' and they are less likely to feel pressure to give the ''right''
answers.

3. *Observation.* If possible, one should observe and participate in the activities of the family and the firm to gain firsthand
knowledge.

4. *Internal Documents.* Annual reports, company and family histories, memoirs, memos, and operational data can be used
to corroborate and expand on data gathered from other sources.
Corporate philosophy, goals, and ideals are often found in these
records. Matters of organization and family life that the family
considers important are often recorded in such documents.

5. *External Documents.* Industry publications, newspaper
reports, company histories, and other external sources of data
can be invaluable. They give the outsider's views of the family
business and therefore can be used to either corroborate or question what has been gathered from inside sources.

6. *Questionnaires.* Although questionnaires are of limited
benefit in mapping a culture, they can be useful to test hypotheses or gather data about attitudes after a preliminary study has
been completed.

The data-gathering process is much like detective work. There are many sources of data and each one needs to be explored. However, it is often difficult to determine which source will be the best one or where key insights will be gained until data collection actually begins.

Sorting the Data. After asking a series of questions and looking at a variety of sources of data, one comes up with a voluminous amount of information about the business, the family, and the board of directors. The data generally form a kind of jigsaw puzzle or riddle that now must be "solved." For some, particularly those in the business, gathering and piecing together such data can be quite threatening, for it exposes many weaknesses and shortcomings. It gets close to the heart of many of the key problems. But it must be done, for without such information, understanding and solving major problems are difficult indeed.

Making sense of such a vast array of data is probably the most difficult stage in the process. We have found that the seven categories of culture are useful in sorting the data (see Chapter Two). For example, after looking at the data gathered, one might ask: What do these data tell me about relationships in the board, the family, and the firm? What seems to be their orientation toward the environment, time, or the nature of truth? Are people trusted or distrusted? What criteria are used to reward and judge people?

Creating a "culture map" is a useful way to organize the analysis. This can be done by preparing charts for the business, the family, and the board that sort the data and map the various levels of culture in the relevant categories. With such maps, the cultural configuration of the firm can be deciphered. An example of a "business culture map" is presented in Table 2, which depicts the cultural pattern of the Brown Corporation during the tenure of John Brown, Sr. The pattern reflected a highly autocratic, secretive business that favored family members.

The reader will note, that not all seven categories were used. In this case, we did not have sufficient data to determine with confidence the "human activity" and "time" orientations. Loose ends are always a part of such an analysis. Some categories may not be used; new categories may be generated. The seven

Table 2. Culture Map of the Brown Corporation.

Category	Artifacts	Perspectives	Values	Assumptions
Nature of relationships	Stories about John, Sr., as a charismatic leader and authority figure Activities such as field day, fishing, clambakes Employees use company equipment for personal needs Jokes about firings Pictures with founder treasured by employees	John, Sr., "takes care" of his employees in return for their loyalty and obedience Deference should be given to those in authority	Security Loyalty Obedience Authority-based status system	The founder holds all power and authority
Human nature	Founder's wife keeps the books, family signs all checks Nonfamily members kept out of decisions and information Stock-fight stories Close supervision	The family should control the key information and make all important decisions Employees should be closely supervised and follow orders	Secrecy Low trust of nonfamily members, particularly those outside the community	Nonfamily members are basically untrustworthy

Table 2. Culture Map of the Brown Corporation, Cont'd.

Category	Artifacts	Perspectives	Values	Assumptions
Environment	Company develops new hydraulic trucks John, Sr., buys one of the first IBM computers Management innovations such as paid vacations Stories about commitment to the work ethic	New ideas should be encouraged and tested Hard work will be rewarded	Innovation Creativity Work ethic	Humans can and should master the environment
Nature of truth	John, Sr., makes all key decisions Ritual of employees asking John, Sr., what to do each day before beginning work	John, Sr., does and should control all key information and make all important decisions	Centralized decision making Authority determines the right to make decisions	"Truth" resides in the founder
Universalism	Family members given key positions John, Jr., groomed to be the next president	Family members should control key functions in the firm	Family membership is an important asset for gaining power and influence	Particularism— family members are given preference

categories are designed to stimulate thinking and provide some guidance as to the kinds of assumptions that might underlie the culture, but they should not become a straitjacket to limit possibilities or inhibit further exploration. Sort and map the data at the various levels of culture in each category as best you can, and the cultural patterns will become more apparent.

Inside/Outside Teams. There are many questions to ask and answer, and much data to gather to complete a picture of the culture of a family firm. Before any analysis, however, putting together the research team is essential. Since the core assumptions of culture are tacit in nature, members of the family or others in the firm may not be able to articulate them. Thus a process of *joint inquiry*, involving both company insiders and external consultants or analysts, is generally necessary to raise the assumptions to a level where they can be analyzed. It is unlikely that either insiders alone or outsiders alone will be able to decipher the cultural pattern. To do this, Schein (1984) suggests: "The insider must be a representative of the culture and must be interested in disclosing his or her own basic assumptions to test whether they are in fact cultural prototypes. This process works best if one acts from observations that puzzle the outsider or that seem like anomalies because the insider's assumptions are most easily surfaced if they are contrasted to the assumptions that the outsider initially holds about what is observed" (p. 13).

An inside/outside team that is able to analyze the data together helps to protect against one another's biases and allows an exchange of ideas that helps both insiders and outsiders better understand the culture they are investigating.

Some Problems of Data Gathering. As we conclude this discussion on assessing cultural patterns, a few notes of caution are in order. First, one problem is that multiple cultures may be embedded in the family firm system. Different perspectives, values, and assumptions are not uncommon; care must be taken to outline the boundaries and "overlaps" between cultures. Often the core problems of a family firm are the result of a clash between family members or employees with different cultural orientations. Therefore it is important to ask interviewees to name individuals or groups with different opinions. The research team may then find themselves creating a number of cultural maps, particularly for the business.

Second, discrepancies between the espoused values and actual behavior are common. For example, Thomas Watson's "Think" motto was ostensibly designed to promote individual initiative among his subordinates. But most of Watson's behaviors emphasized just the opposite—conformity. A researcher who relies solely on statements that espouse a certain ideology can be easily misled. With a system of "checks" on the interview data, a list of "actual" versus "intended" behaviors can be generated.

Finally, cultural studies are hard to disguise: the data are generally about specific people engaging in specific behaviors. Care must be taken to protect interviewees, as well as the organization itself, if the sources of the data are to be kept anonymous. Family firms are notorious for keeping secrets in the family and away from the public eye. Gaining access to the relevant sources of data, let alone deciphering the cultural pattern, is no easy task.

The cultural approach to studying family firms forces one to push deeper, to probe behind the facade and get at the heart of what often are complex issues. The first step in managing change—assessing the cultural patterns of a family, a business, and a board of directors—is not easy. At times it is a rather messy process. But insights gained from such an analysis allow us to better understand the firm's and family's behavior, past and present, and to diagnose those obstacles that hinder both firm and family from reaching their potential.

Step 2. Identify Problems

After assessing the cultural patterns, identifying the major problems is the next step. First, the current problems plaguing the business should be identified. The second step, often more important, is to identify the problems that are likely to come up in the future. To manage change successfully requires the family to focus on both current *and* future problems and plan accordingly.

Certain cultural configurations make it difficult for a family to make successful transitions. Anticipating and planning for these problems is all the more important. For example, if the family knows that leadership succession must occur soon, plans should be developed to ensure that the conditions for managing a successful transition are present. The family should have a plan in place for contingencies such as the illness or death of the founder.

Step 3. Select a Change Strategy

Once the assessment and problem-identification phases are completed, the next step is to articulate clearly the goals of change. To do this, those who will initiate the change should envision what the family, the business, and the board will look like after the change has taken place. For example, they might envision a family firm where:

1. Family members are well trained and prepared to assume leadership roles, in contrast to one where there is little or no training and development.
2. The strategy of the firm is well articulated and adaptable to the demands of the marketplace.
3. Family members have a shared vision of the future.
4. Relationships in the family are based on trust, love, and mutual respect, in contrast to hostility and conflict.
5. Family and nonfamily members are able to collaborate in decision making. Information is shared and authority delegated.
6. There is high commitment to fulfill the organization's mission.
7. Adequate planning has been done to deal with any foreseeable emergencies.
8. The board of directors not only provides insight and direction on the firm's major problems, but helps mediate and manage conflict.

These are just a few of many positive outcomes that a family firm might want to achieve as a result of their efforts to manage change. Until the goals of the change program are clearly defined, selecting the right strategy is a difficult task;

managers cannot decide how to get somewhere if they do not know where they are going. Once the current problems have been assessed and a clear vision of the future articulated, a change strategy can be chosen that will help make the transition from where the family firm is to where it wants to be.

Change Strategies for Common Problems

Problems in family firms range from those that are intensely personal to those that have implications for the entire family and business. These problems often have different causes and therefore require different change strategies. In Table 3, we have listed many of the common problems that afflict family business. They have been collected into four general categories: individual, interpersonal, intergroup, and organizational. Possible change strategies to fit each problem type are noted in the last column.

Individual Change Strategies. At an individual level, three different kinds of problems have been highlighted. The most widespread, particularly in paternalistic and authoritarian family firms, is a lack of awareness by founders or other leaders of the impact of their personal style on the family and the business. Unwittingly they may exacerbate the very problems they are trying to solve. One founder, who was highly confrontive when he received bad news, was surprised that many close advisers failed to alert him to serious problems. They felt that it was too risky, too painful to confront the founder with anything but positive information.

Several things can be done to deal with the "awareness" problem. Two initial steps are data-feedback interventions or "sensing meetings" (see Chapter Four). Data-feedback interventions require the family to gather data about themselves and the business. Sensing meetings involve having certain members of the family firm, usually those at various levels in the company who have access to important information, sit down together in small groups to sort out and describe the sources of their problems. Often a facilitator, someone trusted by all those involved, is useful to manage the discussion, clarify comments,

Table 3. Selecting a Change Strategy.

Problem Level	Problem Type	Change Strategy
Individual	Lack of awareness of personal style, low trust of others, autocratic	Data-feedback; Sensing meetings; Sensitivity groups; Therapy
	Low self-esteem, feelings of inadequacy	Career/life planning; Delegation; Training; Therapy
	Lack of training to assume leadership	Career development; Succession planning; Training
Interpersonal	Interpersonal conflict	Third-party interventions; Role negotiation; Separation
	Powerlessness	Training; Coalition building; Delegation
Intergroup	Intergroup conflict, power struggles	Asset management boards; Goal setting; Third-party interventions; Intergroup
	Lack of cooperation and coordination	conflict interventions; Team building
Organizational	Lack of contingency planning or estate planning	Asset management boards
	No succession plan	Career/succession planning
	Lack of business effectiveness	Strategic planning; Confrontation meetings; Outside/board review

and help the group move to a greater understanding of the effects of a person's behavior.

The leaders of the family firm should initiate this process, and their primary objective should be to learn how their behavior is affecting those in the family firm system. This is rarely done in a family firm, however, because the central problem—lack of awareness—makes it difficult to get people to examine their own behavior or even to realize that anything is wrong. It also can be quite threatening to find out how they are actually perceived by others. Unless the leader is willing to engage in some data gathering, this problem is not likely to be solved.

There are other options, however. We have seen cases where founders or other family members benefited from sensitivity training groups. The aim is to get members of the group to discuss openly their feelings about themselves and others with a skilled facilitator. John Brown, Jr., and his wife found the vehicle of the training group extremely useful for gaining self-insight. Therapy is another, somewhat more extreme, option. If the source of a person's problem appears to lie in some serious, unresolved issues in his or her life, family therapists or other kinds of consultants may be required. Founders or other leaders of family firms are often too proud to admit they have a problem, much less ask for help, so getting them to take this step is not easy. Many of the family firms that we studied, however, could have benefited from a well-trained family therapist or psychologist. If, as is often the case, the individuals refuse to engage in any sort of process to change their behavior, then a final option is to replace them. Given the power structure, this may not be possible in all cases, and it is often painful, but placing them in a position where they can do less damage is preferable to the kinds of problems that can occur if nothing is done.

Feelings of inadequacy and low self-esteem are common among the children, in-laws, and other, less powerful individuals. To deal with this problem, there are several options. In some cases, career counseling or life-planning exercises may help the person get a better perspective of themselves and their careers and make plans to achieve their goals. This planning could be done by outside counselors (such as those in high schools and colleges) as well as leaders of the family business. Delegation and training that allows the individual to take responsibility and achieve results can also be a positive force to enhance self-esteem (see Chapter Four). In the more serious cases, however, therapy may be the only answer to the person's problems (for example, David Bluebird in Chapter Five).

Finally, the lack of preparation of successors must be handled. Creating a career development program that helps to train and develop future leaders is absolutely essential if the business is to survive. This requires the founder and the immediate family to develop criteria to assess and train future leaders.

Interpersonal Change Strategies. As we know, family firms provide fertile ground for interpersonal conflicts. These conflicts, often boiling below the surface, can cripple a family firm—particularly when they impair the family's ability to select and train family members for leadership. In Chapter Five we discussed third-party mediators and role negotiation. To successfully manage these kinds of conflicts requires two things: a willingness on everyone's part to try to work out their differences, and a skilled third party who can sit down with those involved, have them air their differences, and then come to some agreement on managing these differences. If this cannot be done, separating the warring parties by putting them in different functional areas may be the only answer. The problem with this approach, however, is that the conflict is not resolved, only delayed. This tactic should be seen as a short-run solution, while other preparations are being made to manage the conflict.

Powerlessness is another serious problem. It is generally a result of an imbalance of power between two people. As mentioned in Chapter Four, the tactics that can be used to combat this problem are training, delegation, and coalition building by the powerless to enhance their power and influence.

Intergroup Change Strategies. These strategies can be used to manage intergroup conflicts and to improve coordination and cooperation between various factions. Asset management boards can be used as a forum to get diverse groups together. In such a setting, the family and other key people can determine the appropriate goals for the business and the family. Conflict interventions, such as those already suggested plus team building, might be used to build effective family units and work teams (Nielsen, 1972). Team building involves getting ongoing work groups together to analyze and manage the problems they face. The team-building approach generally requires the "team" members to gather data about themselves and their performance (much like Step 1 of the change process), diagnose their problems, and develop a change strategy. Often individual and interpersonal problems are confronted and solved in team-building sessions (Dyer, 1977).

In general, the key to managing intergroup conflicts is to have group members willing to work together and to have a skilled and trusted third party who can help them surface, analyze, and solve the problems they are facing.

Organizational Change Strategies. Some problems affect the entire family firm system—a lack of planning for contingencies, no succession planning, and a lack of business effectiveness. The problems of planning can be managed by setting up boards, committees, or some other mechanism (maybe the founder alone with a few trusted advisers) to plan for the future. The process of gathering data, making decisions, and then sharing the decisions is often more important than the actual plan that emerges. If members of the family firm are not a part of the planning process, there is likely to be much confusion and little commitment to the plan.

When profits are declining, markets shrinking, employees unhappy, or any number of similar problems, the effectiveness of the business is undermined. To analyze these kinds of problems often requires gathering data from outside sources. Outside board members, advisers, or consultants might be called in to help provide some insight about the firm's ailments. Internally, the family should reevaluate the products, the markets, and the technology used to manufacture and distribute those products. Confrontation meetings can be used to gather data from employees and surface the major problems. Once data have been gathered, the family can begin to develop strategic plans to improve products, markets, or technologies that will give the business a competitive advantage. The keys to solving significant organizational problems are developing a set of criteria that alerts the family when the business is not performing as it should and having the people and mechanisms available to gather data quickly to pinpoint the sources of the problem.

Managing Change in Owens, Inc.: A Case Study

One example of a leader of a family business attempting to initiate change is Nicholas Owens of Owens, Inc. (fictional names). Owens, Inc. is a diversified business offering several product lines and services. The business was founded by Nicholas' father, John Owens, who built the firm into a highly successful enterprise. As Nicholas and his younger brother Tyler grew older, they began working in the business; eventually John brought them in as equal partners. John's two daughters, Angela and Glenda, were never thought of as potential owners or managers.

In 1970, John died suddenly of a heart attack. Nicholas, the oldest son, assumed command; he has been the company president for the past fifteen years. The company has continued to expand and grow, but recently a number of problems have emerged:

1. Tyler dislikes taking orders from his brother since they are, in theory, equal partners. Tyler is thinking about splitting up the business so he can run his own company without interference.
2. The daughters feel that they have been treated inequitably. The brothers get large salaries, ownership, and live in relative luxury, while they feel like second-class citizens.
3. Nicholas seems unaware of a number of these problems; when asked, he says that all is going well. Yet he feels uncomfortable about his relationship with his brother and sisters but cannot pinpoint the reason. He sees himself as being open to influence; other family members see him as very autocratic.
4. There are a number of children in the third generation who will be old enough to join the business in the next few years. Little thought has been given to the selection, training, and development of these family members for management positions.

These problems have emerged in a business culture that is highly paternalistic and a family that is conflicted, and in the absence of a board that can provide advice and insight—not uncommon problems for a family firm with this kind of cultural configuration. The problems cover each of the four levels—individual, interpersonal, intergroup, and organizational. Nicholas envisions a future where he and his brother are working cooperatively together, his sisters are not dissatisfied with their positions in the family, and the most competent family members are being groomed for future leadership. To accomplish this will require several actions:

1.　An asset management board of family members needs to be created to discuss the equity problem. A consultant or respected family adviser would be used to facilitate the discussion.
2.　Nicholas and his brother need to clarify expectations and roles. This could be done with the help of a skilled third party.
3.　Nicholas needs feedback and information regarding his performance. The firm currently has only a "paper" board. A search needs to be made for outside advisers or board members who can counsel Nicholas and help him gain some insight into his own behavior.
4.　A succession planning system outlining the criteria of selection, training, and advancement for the third generation needs to be developed. This could be done by members of the asset management board with selected nonfamily managers and advisers, whose input would be necessary for any plan to work.

While he realizes many of the difficulties in carrying out such a plan, Nicholas believes that without such action the future of the business and the family is not bright—particularly since he wants the business to remain a family concern.

Step 4. Implement the Strategy

To implement any change strategy requires the cooperation and commitment of those who must carry out the strategy. Resistance to change is especially strong in family firms, since certain family members may see change as threatening their power and security. Founders resist change because they see it as the harbinger of decline and death. The family may resist examining the difficult and delicate issues surrounding interpersonal relationships, succession planning, and ownership distribution. But if a change strategy is to be successful, these obstacles must be overcome.

The first step in generating commitment and overcoming resistance to change is to answer two questions: How willing are family members (and nonfamily employees, if they are to be involved) to change? How capable are they of carrying out the change effort? The first question implies that family members feel some need to change, some reason for undergoing the stress that often accompanies change. One reason we generally see change taking place during crisis periods is that is when people feel a strong need to change. If the family sees no need to change, any change strategy is likely to fail. In the Owens case, unless both brothers feel the need to change their relationship and work out their differences, the chances for implementing a successful change strategy are greatly reduced. Thus stimulating the need—by sharing data, by exposing the family to the dangers of complacency, or by providing feedback that the business and family have some serious problems—is the initial step. Once people feel the need to change, the chances for success are increased dramatically.

The next step is to determine the family members' ability to follow through with the strategy. This includes both the power to make things happen and the skill needed to manage the change process. If a "critical mass" of key individuals does not support the strategy, plans should be made to get their support (Beckhard and Harris, 1977). Key individuals should be targeted and strategies developed to influence them. In the experience of most family firms, the founders or family leaders with the controlling ownership are the persons most important to any change effort. Without their support, the change effort is doomed. However, history demonstrates that founders resist change, even in the face of overwhelming data that indicates they *should* change. Strategies must be developed to influence the key figures and gain their support. Once the key people are committed, and the right people with the appropriate skills and knowledge are in place to carry out the plan, specific projects can be assigned.

Step 5. Evaluate the Strategy

The last step in the process involves evaluation. This is not easy—many of the outcomes of the change effort are difficult to measure. For example, how do we determine whether interpersonal relationships have improved or intergroup conflict minimized? But, somehow, evaluations must be done.

Setting short-term, intermediate, and long-term goals is an important part of the change process. The goals should be as "measurable" as possible, and a time frame developed. In many cases, the asset management board, or other groups working on the problem, should meet at predetermined times to discuss their progress. Similarly, individuals with interpersonal problems need to sit down with one another and assess how their relationship has changed as the result of a particular change strategy. Without such monitoring, the initial excitement generated from a change strategy often wears off and the change effort dies. Periodic evaluations help to assess progress, make corrections where necessary, and reinforce the change strategy. In the Nebeker family described in Chapter Five, the change strategy would have been much more effective if the family had had periodic reviews with the consultant to keep the change effort alive. As it turned out, the consultant did not follow up and the family reverted back to their old patterns.

To summarize, the steps involved in managing change are given below.

1. Gather data to assess the cultural patterns of the business, the family, and the governing board(s).
2. Identify current and potential problems stemming from the cultural configuration.
3. Select a change strategy.
4. Implement the change strategy.
5. Evaluate the effectiveness of the change effort.

Nine

ᚴᚬᛋᚿᚴᚬᛋᚿᚴᚬᛋᚿᚴᚬᛋᚿᚴᚬᛋᚿᚴᚬᛋᚿᚴᚬᛋᚿ

The Twelve Signs
of a Healthy Firm

In this book we have described a variety of family firm cultures, the problems those cultures create, and techniques for managing those problems. We have seen that the issues facing the manager of a family business change over the four stages of a firm's life cycle. In Stages 1 and 2 the key problems surround the founder's ability to plan for the future, to understand his weaknesses and compensate for them, to adapt to changing business conditions, and to prepare the family and business for a smooth transition to the next generation. The manager in Stage 3 is often confronted with family and business conflicts that were not found during the founder's tenure because family interests often diverge in the second generation. Managing those conflicts and creating a "collective vision" is the core problem for second-generation leaders. In Stage 4, as the company goes public or brings in professional management, the leader of the family firm is concerned with maintaining basic family and business values in light of new ownership and management structures.

In the cases we studied, however, it is apparent that most family firms do not manage these problems well. In this chapter we will summarize the major pitfalls that ensnare family firms and present some final suggestions for managing the change process.

The Warning Signs

In the family firms that we studied, there were common "danger" signs that warned of impending disaster. These warning signs can be found at any stage of the family firm's devel-

opment. The following questions can help managers detect a
problem:

1. Are the family and its leaders aware of the problems and
    tradeoffs that they are now facing or will face in the future?
2. Has the family planned for future family and business
    needs?
3. Is there a well-thought-out management succession plan,
    and has it been communicated to the relevant parties?
4. Has the family developed an ownership succession plan
    that complements the management succession plan?
5. Do the leader and the successors have an interdependent
    relationship?
6. Does an effective training program exist for the future
    leaders of the business?
7. Do members of the firm (both family and nonfamily) share
    similar views of equity and competence?
8. Do family members work together collaboratively to solve
    problems?
9. Has the family created successful mechanisms for manag-
    ing conflict?
10. Are there high levels of trust among family members as
    well as among family and nonfamily employees?
11. Do the leaders have feedback mechanisms (outside board
    members, consultants, effectiveness measures) to tell them
    when they're off course or are ineffective?
12. Does the family have a "balanced perspective" when mak-
    ing tradeoffs between family needs and business needs?

The experience of the family firms in our panel indicates
that if any of these questions is answered "No," then the firm
can be in jeopardy. If the family can answer each question
"Yes," the prospects for the future are bright. However, if a
family fails to plan for the future or fosters inequities and conflicts that are not resolved, or if they are not aware of the effects of their behavior and can make course corrections, the
outlook for the family firm is bleak.

Furthermore, we have seen that some of the more
common cultural configurations in family firms are at the root

of most problems. In family firms where authority was highly centralized in the leader, family members and employees were either in conflict or highly dependent upon the leader for guidance, and there was little or no review or support from board members. The family firm often cannot muster the resources necessary to solve its problems and manage a successful transition. If leaders of family firms find themselves with these kinds of cultural patterns—or others that create similar problems—action must be taken quickly.

Managing the Process

Chapter Eight outlined some change strategies that can be used to manage the problems of a family firm. One of the more common pitfalls that prevent leaders of family businesses from managing change successfully is their tendency to be too "solution oriented." What does that mean? Let us take the case of a leader of a large family firm who has six children and wants to begin planning for succession. The children of this chief executive are still too young to join the business, but he wants the answer to the question: Whom should I choose as my successor? He has spent considerable time with a consultant on the matter. The problem is, he has asked the wrong question. The question should not be *who* will be my successor, but *how* should my successor be chosen? The leader wants the consultant to help him decide which child will succeed him, so he can lay the issue aside and focus on other problems. He wants a "quick fix."

But without developing and managing a *process* for selecting a successor, any decision is likely to be fruitless, even counterproductive. The leader's spouse may be unhappy with the choice, the children not chosen may resent being left out, and nonfamily employees may question the wisdom of the decision.

To develop a process for managing this problem, the leader might:

1. Gather data from family members, the business, and board members to determine the needs, desires, and aspirations of the various parties.
2. Select a change mechanism, such as an asset management

board or some other forum, to continue a dialogue with family and nonfamily members about the succession question.

3. Use the board to clarify expectations, set goals, and provide support and training for family or nonfamily members who are a part of the succession plan.
4. Evaluate performance, give feedback, and provide guidance to potential successors.

These four steps do not provide an instant solution to the problem of succession. Instead, they force the leader to manage his world proactively, to create the conditions to ensure a good decision is made when the time comes. This is clearly more work than merely selecting the "right" person, but the chances for a successful transition are enhanced when the leader actively manages the process.

"Enlightened" Leadership: The Key to Success

While many of our examples have highlighted the weaknesses of leaders of family firms, we also discovered a number of highly successful leaders. To illustrate their attributes, let us briefly look at the leadership style of Thomas Garcia (fictional name), head of a multimillion-dollar family conglomerate in Latin America. Garcia founded his business (primarily life insurance) as a means of helping his fellow countrymen obtain adequate insurance to cover their basic needs. He is committed to carrying out this "mission" and has selected and socialized his managers (both family and professional managers) in an attempt to continue those values into the future. He has also expanded successfully into new areas as conditions in the business environment have changed.

He has also created an asset management board to teach his children their ownership and management roles. One of his sons, who is interested in the business, was given the opportunity to develop his management skills by operating his own construction firm, which is part of the conglomerate. His other children are not in the management of the business, but he has included them in making decisions about the ownership of the firm and has encouraged them in their own careers. He has been willing to collaborate with and support family members and non-family managers, while still providing the vision and driving force behind the business.

He has had a difficult time confronting the succession question. He initially tried to avoid the issue, but realized that he was just "playing games." He believes that in order to ensure continuity of his business and his family, he must begin to develop and manage a succession plan *now*. He believes he should include his wife in this process. In the past, he had excluded her from virtually all information about the business. Taking these steps has not been easy. He has had to struggle continually with the problem of delegating power to others. He does not want to give up all the benefits of the founder role. Yet he realizes that he must prepare for the time when he can no longer run the business. To that end, he has begun to cultivate interests outside the business. When he retires, he plans to teach part time at a local university and remain active in civic affairs. He will undoubtedly spend more time with his family, particularly his grandchildren.

Mr. Garcia is, in many ways, one of the more "enlightened" founders we encountered. He recognizes the forces within him and around him that push him to avoid dealing with some very difficult and threatening issues. Yet he has been able to work through these issues—with the support of his family—and now feels confident that the process he has put in place to manage succession will preserve his business, help his family, and provide him with a meaningful life after he retires.

Conclusion

The pitfalls that managers of family firms encounter as they attempt to meet the needs of the family and business are many. The experience of most family firms is one of frustration, conflict, and unfulfilled dreams. The problems facing a family business cannot be completely avoided—therefore they must be managed. To manage these problems requires enlightened leadership. Leaders of family firms must (1) recognize the cultural patterns of their business, their family, and their board of directors; (2) understand both the strengths and weaknesses of their cultures and anticipate potential problems; (3) create structures and mechanisms to manage their problems; and (4) initiate and manage the process of change. This road is not easy—and, unfortunately, not well traveled—but it must be taken if leaders of family firms are to ensure the continuity of their businesses and the well-being of their families.

Cultural Assumptions in Family Firms

Assumptions About Relationships

In most family firms, we have found that relationships in the family, the business, and the board are hierarchical in nature. One family member, typically the founder, is assumed to be the undisputed leader and authority figure. The rest of the family, employees, and board members are subservient to him or her. A small minority of family firms, such as W. L. Gore and Associates, tend to foster more collateral or group-oriented relationships. In such organizations status and hierarchy are discounted and democratic ideals are emphasized. Other family firms have individualistic relationships. Such firms are characterized by competition among family members and employees for positions, wealth, and status. People are assumed to be seeking individual goals and rewards rather than the objectives of the organization or the group.

Assumptions About Human Nature

This category concerns whether people are assumed to be basically good and trustworthy, or whether they are seen as dishonest and not worthy of confidence. In some firms, such as Du Pont, family members had deep feelings of distrust for other family members, and this assumption was at the core of many of the family disputes. Other families tend to be more neutral along this dimension—at times showing trust, at other times great distrust. Still others have created a highly trusting atmosphere within their families and businesses. A climate of trust makes collaboration on problem solving much easier.

Assumptions About the Nature of Truth

This dimension concerns how members of a family firm gather data about their world and make decisions. In some family businesses, the tendency is to assume that the founder or some other family member has all the relevant information, expertise, and power to make all the major decisions. Decision-making authority rests in the hands of only one or two individuals. Much like small children, the family and nonfamily employees trust the authority figures to make the right decisions for them. In other firms, however, decision making is based on the belief that no one person has all the answers. In the GEM Corporation, for example, the founder Bill Henry (fictional names) believes that knowledge is discovered and best decisions made when employees are encouraged to debate and negotiate a solution among themselves. This assumption forces employees to develop their own ideas and collaborate with others to solve problems.

Assumptions About the Environment

Assumptions along this dimension have to do with what the group perceives is the correct way to handle problems posed by the environment. For those in the business, this generally involves how they answer the following questions:

1. What business are we in and what are our goals?
2. How do we succeed in this business?
3. Who are our competitors and what is our competitive advantage?
4. What specific strategies and tactics do we need to design and implement to help us achieve our goals?

Depending on the kind of business, there are many possible answers to these questions. However, businesses tend to have one of three orientations: (1) a proactive stance, which focuses on creating new markets and opportunities; (2) a "harmonizing" response—taking a niche in a market and filling it without expanding into other areas; or (3) a "reacting" stance, merely responding to environmental forces because leaders of the business feel they have little control over their world. Such assumptions underpin the strategy of the firm and often determine its success or failure.

Family and board orientations along this dimension differ from the business in terms of goals, but they still hold similar assumptions about their ability to control external forces. For example, some families believe they can plan for and control many of the problems related to leadership succession. Others feel that they are victims of circumstance, and that any action on their part is doomed to failure; therefore they do nothing. Such assumptions have a profound impact on behavior.

Assumptions About Universalism

This dimension concerns how people are granted rewards and status. In groups with a particularistic orientation, status is awarded on the basis of family membership, age, sex, birth order, or some other criterion not related to performance. In many family businesses, these criteria determine one's position in the family and the firm. In universalistic groups, however, everyone is afforded the same opportunity. Performance is what counts, not family ties or connections.

Assumptions along this dimension often create a number of role conflicts. For example, in most families, family members are deemed to have intrinsic worth regardless of performance. Failures are overlooked and prodigal sons and daughters are accepted back into the fold. But in many businesses the main criterion for acceptance is performance. Poor performers are disciplined and those who fail are fired. Such assumptions directly contradict one another. This can create problems when some family members assume that family connections should be the criteria for success while others feel that all those working in the business should be treated equally. When assessing the culture of a family firm, it is important to understand these differences, for they are often the key to many of the problems.

Assumptions About Time

Assumptions about time also vary in the business, family, and the governing board. Some groups tend to be oriented to the past. Traditions are followed implicitly and provide the guide for future action. Other family firms seem to be concerned only about the present. They are oriented to meeting today's needs and goals. Other firms tend to be more future oriented. They spend a great deal of time developing plans and strategies that would help them meet challenges in the future.

Assumptions About the Nature of Activity

This dimension is related closely to the universalism category since it concerns the kinds of individual activities and developmental processes that are valued. Most of the family businesses we studied had a "doing" orientation. Employees and family members were rewarded for getting the job done; little attention was paid to how the job was accomplished or whether the person performing the task benefited from it. This is in stark contrast to those firms that emphasized the development of the individual as a primary concern of management. Getting the job done was important, but so was developing and training family members and employees for increased responsibility. In a few firms, we found that people were assumed to be basically passive and not easily motivated. Little attention was paid to either getting the job done or improving people's skills. Apathy and frustration were generally the results of such a belief.

References

Adizes, I. "Organizational Passages—Diagnosing and Treating Life Cycle Problems of Organizations." *Organizational Dynamics*, Summer 1979, pp. 3–25.

"All in the Family." *Time*, Oct. 14, 1985, pp. 67, 68.

Allyn, S. C. *My Half Century with NCR*. New York: McGraw-Hill, 1967.

Barnes, L. B., and Hershon, S. A. "Transferring Power in the Family Business." *Harvard Business Review*, July-Aug. 1976, pp. 105–114.

Becker, H. S., Geer, B., Hughes, E. C., and Strauss, A. L. *Boys in White*. New Brunswick, N.J.: Transaction Books, 1961.

Beckhard, R. "The Confrontation Meeting." *Harvard Business Review*, 1967, *45* (2), 149–155.

Beckhard, R., and Dyer, W. G., Jr. "Managing Continuity in the Family-Owned Business." *Organizational Dynamics*, Summer 1983a, pp. 5–12.

Beckhard, R., and Dyer, W. G., Jr. "SMR Forum: Managing Change in the Family Firm—Issues and Strategies." *Sloan Management Review*, 1983b, *24* (3), 59–65.

Beckhard, R., and Harris, R. T. *Organizational Transitions: Managing Complex Change*. Reading, Mass.: Addison-Wesley, 1977.

Bem, D. J. *Beliefs, Attitudes, and Human Affairs*. Monterey, Calif.: Brooks/Cole, 1970.

Berle, A. A., and Means, G. C. *The Modern Corporation and Private Property*. San Diego, Calif.: Harcourt Brace Jovanovich, 1968.

Brown, J. "Dunckley Music Company." Unpublished Case Study, Brigham Young University, 1985a.

Brown, J. "Mr. and Mrs. Jones, Inc." Unpublished Case Study, Brigham Young University, 1985b.

Buckner, K. "The Western Freight Company." Unpublished Case Study, Brigham Young University, 1985.

Carruth, E. "Genesco Comes to Judgment," *Fortune,* July 1975, pp. 108–180.

Chandler, A. D., Jr. *Strategy and Structure.* Cambridge, Mass.: MIT Press, 1962.

Chandler, A. D., Jr. *The Visible Hand.* Boston: Harvard University Press, 1977.

Chandler, A. D., Jr., and Salisbury, S. *Pierre S. Du Pont and the Making of the Modern Corporation.* New York: Harper & Row, 1971.

Checketts, A. G. "Cases of Second Generation Family Businesses." Unpublished Case Studies, Brigham Young University, 1985.

Cook, J. "When a Family Falls Out." *Forbes,* Nov. 1, 1976, pp. 32, 33.

Cray, E. *Levi's.* Boston: Houghton Mifflin, 1978.

Cray, E. *Chrome Colossus.* New York: McGraw-Hill, 1980.

Crowther, S. *John H. Patterson: Pioneer in Industrial Welfare.* New York: Doubleday, 1923.

Danco, L. A. *Beyond Survival: A Business Owner's Guide for Success.* Cleveland, Ohio: University Press, 1982.

Deal, T. E., and Kennedy, A. A. *Corporate Cultures: The Rites and Rituals of Corporate Life.* Reading, Mass.: Addison-Wesley, 1982.

Dyer, W. G., Jr. *Team Building: Strategies and Alternatives.* Reading, Mass.: Addison-Wesley, 1977.

Dyer, W. G., Jr. "Culture in Organizations: A Case Study and Analysis." Working paper no. 1279–82, Sloan School of Management, Massachusetts Institute of Technology, Feb. 1982.

Dyer, W. G., Jr. "Cutural Evolution in Organizations: The Case of a Family Owned Firm." Unpublished doctoral dissertation, Sloan School of Management, Massachusetts Institute of Technology, 1984a.

Dyer, W. G., Jr. "Organizational Culture: Analysis and Change." In W. G. Dyer, Jr. (ed.), *Strategies for Managing Change.* Reading, Mass.: Addison-Wesley, 1984b.

Dyer, W. G., Jr. "The Cycle of Cultural Evolution in Organizations." In R. H. Kilmann, M. J. Saxton, R. Serpa, and

Associates (eds.), *Gaining Control of the Corporate Culture*. San Francisco: Jossey-Bass, 1985.

"Fiat Chairman Giovanni Agnelli, A Risk Taker, Vows to Continue Fight for Firm's Survival." *Wall Street Journal*, Feb. 28, 1985, p. 36.

Galbraith, J. K. *The New Industrial State*. Boston: Houghton Mifflin, 1971.

Greiner, L. E. "Evolution and Revolution as Organizations Grow." *Harvard Business Review*, July-Aug. 1972, pp. 37–46.

Hershon, S. A. "The Problem of Management Succession in Family Businesses." Unpublished dissertation, Harvard University, 1975.

Hollander, B. "Family Owned Business as a System." Unpublished dissertation, University of Pittsburgh, 1982.

Homans, G. C. *The Human Group*. San Diego, Calif.: Harcourt Brace Jovanovich, 1950.

House, R. "A 1976 Theory of Charismatic Leadership." In J. G. Hunt and L. L. Larson (eds.), *Leadership: The Cutting Edge*. Carbondale: Southern Illinois Press, 1977.

Kanter, R. M. *Men and Women of the Corporation*. New York: Basic Books, 1977.

Kepner, E. "The Family and the Firm: A Coevolutionary Perspective." *Organizational Dynamics*, 1983, *12* (1), 57–70.

Kets de Vries, M.F.R. "The Entrepreneurial Personality: A Person at the Crossroads." *Journal of Management Studies*, 1977, *14*, 34–57.

Kets de Vries, M.F.R., and Miller, D. *The Neurotic Organization: Diagnosing and Changing Counterproductive Styles of Management*. San Francisco: Jossey-Bass, 1984.

Kluckhohn, C. "The Concept of Culture." In D. Lerner and H. D. Lasswell (eds.), *The Policy Sciences*. Palo Alto, Calif.: Stanford University Press, 1951.

Kluckhohn, F. R., and Strodtbeck, F. L. *Variations in Value Orientations*. New York: Harper & Row, 1961.

Levinson, H. "Conflicts That Plague Family Business." *Harvard Business Review*, Mar.-Apr. 1971, pp. 90–98.

Levinson, H. "Consulting With Family Businesses: What to Look For, What to Look Out For." *Organizational Dynamics*, *1983*, *12* (1), 71–80.

Lewis, M. B. "Surviving Quarterback of the Estate Planning Team." *Trusts and Estates,* Oct. 1978, p. 694.

Light, D., Jr. "Surface Data and Deep Structure: Observing the Organization of Professional Training." *Administrative Science Quarterly,* 1979, *24* (4), 551–559.

"McCardell Starts Things Moving at International Harvester." *Duns Review,* Apr. 1978.

McClelland, D. C. *The Achieving Society.* New York: Free Press, 1961.

McGivern, C. "The Dynamics of Management Succession." *Management Decision.* 1978, *16* (1), 32–42.

McKinnon, P. "Bennett Association (A)." Colgate Darden Graduate School of Administration, University of Virginia, 1983a.

McKinnon, P. "Bennett Association (B)." Colgate Darden School of Administration, University of Virginia, 1983b.

Marcus, S. *Minding the Store.* Boston: Little, Brown, 1974.

Meek, C. "Lab or Management Committee Outcomes: The Jamestown Case." In W. Woodworth, C. Meek, and W. F. Whyte (eds.), *Industrial Democracy.* Beverly Hills, Calif.: Sage, 1985.

Mintzberg, H., and Waters, J. A. "Tracking Strategy in an Entrepreneurial Firm." *Academy of Management Journal,* 1982, *25* (3), 465–499.

Nielsen, E. H. "Understanding and Managing Intergroup Conflict." In J. W. Lorsch and P. R. Lawrence (eds.), *Managing Group and Intergroup Relations.* Homewood, Ill.: Richard D. Irwin and Dorsey Press, 1972.

Nystrom, P. C., and Starbuck, W. H. "To Avoid Organizational Crises, Unlearn." *Organizational Dynamics,* 1984, *12* (4), 53–65.

Orwell, G. *1984.* New York: New American Library, 1949.

Ouchi, W. G. *Theory Z.* Reading, Mass.: Addison-Wesley, 1981.

Parsons, T., and Shils, E. A. (eds.) *Toward a General Theory of Action.* New York: Harper & Row, 1951.

Peay, R. "The Nebeker Family." Unpublished Case Study, Brigham Young University, 1985.

Peters, T. J., and Waterman, R. H., Jr. *In Search of Excellence: Lessons from America's Best-Run Companies.* New York: Harper & Row, 1982.

Pettigrew, A. M. "On Studying Organizational Cultures." *Administrative Science Quarterly,* 1979, *24,* 570–581.

Poe, R. "The SOB's." *Across the Board,* May 1980, pp. 23–33.

Quinn, J. B. *Strategies for Change: "Logical Incrementalism."* Homewood, Ill.: Dow Jones-Irwin, 1980.

Rokeach, M. *The Nature of Human Values.* New York: Free Press, 1973.

Rosenblatt, P. C., de Mik, L., Anderson, R. M., and Johnson, P. A. *The Family in Business.* San Francisco: Jossey-Bass, 1985.

Salomon, R. "Second Thoughts on Going Public." *Harvard Business Review,* Sept.-Oct. 1977, pp. 126–131.

Schein, E. H. "Does Japanese Management Style Have a Message for American Managers?" *Sloan Management Review,* 1981, *23,* 55–68.

Schein, E. H. "The Role of the Founder in Creating Organizational Cultures." *Organizational Dynamics,* 1983, *12* (1), 13–28.

Schein, E. H. "Coming to a New Awareness of Organizational Culture." *Sloan Management Review,* 1984, *25* (2), 3–16.

Schein, E. H. *Organizational Culture and Leadership: A Dynamic View.* San Francisco: Jossey-Bass, 1985.

Selznick, P. *Leadership in Administration.* New York: Harper & Row, 1957,

Trice, H., and Beyer, J. "Charisma and Its Routinization in Two Social Movements." In B. Staw and L. L. Cummings (eds.), *Research in Organizational Behavior.* Greenwich, Conn.: JAI Press, 1985.

Trow, D. B. "Executive Succession in Small Companies." *Administrative Science Quarterly,* Sept. 1961, pp. 228–239.

Walton, R. *Interpersonal Peace Making: Confrontations and Third Party Consultation.* Reading, Mass.: Addison-Wesley, 1969.

Wilkins, A., and Patterson, K. "You Can't Get There From Here: What Will Make Culture Change Projects Fail." In R. H. Kilmann, M. J. Saxton, R. Serpa, and Associates (eds.), *Gaining Control of the Corporate Culture.* San Francisco: Jossey-Bass, 1985.

Zaleznick, A. "Managers and Leaders: Are They Different." *Harvard Business Review,* May-June 1977, pp. 67–78.

Index

A

Adaptation, and change, 54–55
Adizes, I., 4
Advisory culture: of boards, 39–40, 41; in first generation, 68; and transition, 136
Agnelli, G., 129
Allyn, S. C., 15–16, 45–47, 62–63
Anderson, R. M., 35
Arthur Young & Co., 111
Artifacts: as cultural level, 15–17; in culture map, 143–144
Assets, conflicts over, 87–88, 90
Assumptions: alternative, 47–48; categories of, 19–20, 163–166; as cultural level, 18–20; in culture map, 143–144; in family firms, 23

B

Barringer, J. H., 83
Becker, H. S., 17
Beckhard, R., 90, 91, 124, 155
Beliefs, pattern maintenance of, 46–47
Bem, D. J., 19
Bennett, W., 76, 110–112, 115
Bennett Enterprises: cultural change at, 48, 54; culture of, 16, 18; founder culture at, 76; and professional management, 109–112, 115
Bennett family, 109–111
Berle, A. A., 96
Beronio, D., 19
Beyer, J., 60
Blake, R., 31
Bluebird family, 85–86, 151

Boards, governing: advisory culture of, 39–40, 41, 68, 136; cultural patterns in, 37–40; data gathering on, 140–141; expertise of, 135; and founder culture, 67; overseer culture of, 40, 41; paper culture of, 38, 136; and power clarity, 134–135; rubber-stamp culture of, 39, 41, 68, 136; in succeeding generation, 82; transition conditions for, 134–135, 137
Booz Allen & Hamilton, 33
Boss, W., 36
Boss family, 133
Brown, J., 92, 112, 114
Brown, J., Jr., 7–12, 38, 39–40, 44, 78, 87, 106, 135, 144, 150
Brown, J., Sr., 6–9, 11–12, 35, 38, 39–40, 54–55, 71–72, 76–78, 87, 98, 104–105, 132, 142–144
Brown Corporation: cultural change at, 44–45, 47, 48, 50, 54–56; culture map of, 142–144; culture of, 15, 18, 35, 38, 39–40; founder culture at, 68, 71–72, 76–78; life cycle of, 5–13; and professional management, 102–103, 104–105, 106, 108; and public ownership, 98; and succeeding generation, 84, 87, 89–90; and transition, 132, 135
Brown family, 7, 10–11
Buckner, K., 24, 25
Business: cultural patterns in, 22–34; data gathering about, 139–140; founder's involvement with, 124–126; health of, 123–124; interdependence in, 129–131; laissez-faire culture in, 23, 26–29, 83, 136; par-

173